Copyright ©2017 by jonathan schork

All rights reserved. No part of this book may be reproduced in any form or by any means, electronic or mechanical, including photocopying, recording, or by any information storage or retrieval system, without permission in writing from the author.

Published by SM-ARC, inc.,
p.o.box 10691, St. Petersburg, fl 33733

ISBN-13: 978-0-9979212-4-3

ISBN-10: 0-9979212-4-2

Library of Congress 2017909439

The Bathroom Rule:

Ten short plays
by jonathan schork

Table of Contents:

Forward……………………………………………………...iii
1. Sailing With Unsettled Spirits……………..……………1
2. The Audition......……………..…...……..………………19
3. Good Grooming For the Discriminating Gentleman…..45
4. The Commencement Speaker……………………….…75
5. Contraïndications……………………………………...87
6. Vernissage, or, A Short Documentary
    on the Language of Art-speak………………….113
7. The Nightly News…………………………………….139
8. On the Bus…………………………………………….163
9. G_O_O_M_B_A_S!……………………………...……189
10. Last Rights…………………………………..………219

i

Forward~

Have you ever been in the toilet and so desperate to have something to read that you acquainted yourself with the ingredients of shampoo or tooth paste? The bathroom rule is a simple one, and will be understood immediately by everyone who likes to take with them something to read while they conduct their toilet: the best articles and stories are the ones one can finish in the time it takes to eliminate one's stool. Some of you are all business: a classic haiku is too long for you. Some of you will stay until you finish *War and Peace*. For most of us, though, a nice, relaxing movement of ten to twelve minutes seems about right. (I should admit, in the spirit of candour, that I occasionally disappear into the loo with the New York Times

Sunday crossword puzzle, and can get rather caught up in the "War and Peace" of things.)

I may be a bit of a unicorn for the theatre community: I enjoy writing plays, but only as an exercise in dialogue; I enjoy acting immensely, but loathe sitting in the audience; I enjoy a good character arc, but eschew melodrama in my real life; I enjoy directing, but dislike giving orders. It's a conundrum.

When I volunteered with my wife, the late Mary Cooke Hoeft, in the public high school in rural New York State where she taught for 28 years (from which, parenthetically, we had both graduated, some years apart), we became at one point the *de facto* drama department: the kids were willin', but there were no faculty interested in obliging them, and my wife had an aversion to the word "no", and I, being a dutiful husband, helped her whenever she asked. So, we became the *de facto* drama department. We taught Shakespeare in class, we taught Miller & Moliere, & Shaw & Wilde (in secret—shhhh!) & Wilder & Williams. This was part of the curriculum, though, and not a full experience in theatre. When asked, my wife created an after-school drama group to stage a real play. My favorite, I think, was the year we staged *Arsenic & Old Lace*: we had a slightly disagreeable auntie, but a brilliant Jonathan & Dr. Einstein, a perfect *ingénue*, and a scene-stealing Teddy (plus, our "Mr. Spenalzo" wasn't so bad). We did good work, and our students benefitted from it. To my great good fortune, I learned a lot on that stage, not only about the earnest goofiness of kids acting like adults acting, but about the language of theatre.

If you meet a theatre professional, the very first thing they'll inevitably do is credential themselves with all their roles and stages, plays & playwrights, and, very occasionally, their awards (assuming they've won any). I won't presume to do that here—it's tedious. What I will do, however, is invite you to use what follows: ten short plays of no particular significance. All of these are under twelve minutes, meaning you can read one in the time it takes to use the loo. All of them have been read somewhere; some of them have been performed, and a few of them staged. Maybe you'll find something that suits you. Can't get off book? Try Frank N. Stein-Monster in *the Commencement Speaker*, or part of the news crew in *The Nightly News*. Wanna spoof your abrasive director? Try *The Audition*. Try anything you like, and if you feel so inclined, let me know how it went: I love post mortems.

I should extend a little gratitude to some people here, who have been generous enough to stage several of these plays: the *Gulfport*

Community Players, of Gulfport, Florida, led by the determined & talented Eileen Navarro, are beloved in their little ville, and have done some fine work befitting people with passion. I don't go to their performances—as previously mentioned, I take little pleasure in watching a play—but I'm a big fan of their work, and enjoy submitting work for their annual short play fest (which *you* should do, if you're a writer: search for the page at www.gulfportcommunityplayers.org). Anyhow, to them I say, "Thank you."

The most important lesson I ever learned about theatre is the same thing I learned about Burning Man, and about life, and it's this: don't be a spectator; there's no substitute for participating.

~jonathan schork~

1. Sailing With Unsettled Spirits

Synopsis: four sailors lost at sea struggle to get back to their ship, but is it too late: have they already gone down to the sea?

The Cast:

The CAPTAIN, a somewhat pompous commander with flowery speech & a big hat, but not much else.

SEAMEN 1, 2, & 3: just a trio of old salts trying to get home, lacking confidence in their skipper & their own memories.

The Stage: A tiny launch from a distant ship, bobbing on the ocean. (*You can substitute four chairs for the boat!)

ACT I

Scene 1

Four people sit in a small row boat in the water. They are shabbily attired in white & grey rags; the colour extends to their flesh, which is pallid & wan. Three SEAMEN stir the water around them vigorously with improvised paddles whilst the fourth, their CAPTAIN, calls out from his perch in the bow. In the distance, a much larger ship looms, tantalizing near.

CAPTAIN

Row, you dogs! Row like your lives depend on it! Row... row... row... row...

The three SEAMEN splash furiously, but it is apparent the little boat is not moving.

Alright, stop! Stop, damn your hides, stop!

The rowing halts abruptly; everyone looks around, bewildered.

SEAMAN 1

> What's the matter, Cap?

CAPTAIN

> Well, isn't it apparent? Our ship is over there, whilst we are not. We need to be over there, with our ship, before she leaves without us.

SEAMAN 2

> Beggin' yer pardon, Cap, but we've been paddlin' for days, an' we don't never get no closer that we is right now.

CAPTAIN

> ... *Sir*.

SEAMAN 2

> Sir?

CAPTAIN

> Than we is right now, *sir*. You forgot to say *sir*: I am still the Captain of this tub, crewman.

SEAMAN 2

> Yes, sir. Than we is right now, *sir*.

CAPTAIN

> (*exasperated*)

> I thank you, crewman, for that brilliant declaration of the painfully obvious. In the hereafter, perhaps *you'll* be the Captain.

SEAMAN 3

> We've been such a long time in this launch, I can scarce remember m' bunk.

SEAMAN 2

> Yeah, an' when's the last time we had a hot meal?

SEAMAN 1

> ... Or a cup o' grog?

SEAMAN 2

> It's just a plain bad idea to get marooned in a launch without grog or a hot meal...

SEAMAN 3

> ... Or a bunk.

CAPTAIN

> Gentlemen, please: if we had grog, a hot meal, & our quarters, we wouldn't be in this wretched little dingy; we'd be on our ship. Notwithstanding all that, we are sailors: we don't whinge, we row!

SEAMAN 1

> But Captain, the rowin' don't seem to be workin' much.

CAPTAIN

> And does the whinging seem to be working better?

SEAMAN 1

> I liked our old ship.

SEAMAN 2

> Me, too. She weren't the prettiest barque on the ocean, nor the fastest...

SEAMAN 3

> No, she surely weren't the fastest.

CAPTAIN

> Why are you talking about her as if she were deceased? She's right there. We could almost swim to her.

SEAMAN 2

> Oh, I don't know 'bout that, Cap. I don't know how to swim.

SEAMAN 1

> Nor me, neither.

SEAMAN 2 & 3

    No, sir. Seems like none of us can swim.

CAPTAIN

    Yes, & you miss your grog & your bunks & your hot food. So, let's put our backs into it and row like our lives depend on it. Row! Row!

        The SEAMEN start churning the water again furiously with their makeshift paddles but slowly lose their enthusiasm and momentum: the launch has not moved.

CAPTAIN

    Come on, sailors! Don't give up now. Let's put our backs into it.

SEAMAN 1

    Begging your pardon, sir, but I don't rightly see as how you're puttin' *your* back to anything.

CAPTAIN

    Well, I'm the Captain: I put my back to the work *mentally*. My job is to inspire you lazy dogs. Surely you don't expect me actually to row?

        The SEAMEN all nod in agreement. They stare away

>   *from each other awkwardly for*
>   *a few moments.*

SEAMAN 1

>   Say, who made you capt'n, anyhow?
>   You don't seem no diff'rent than
>   us.

CAPTAIN

>   Don't be ridiculous: I speak much
>   better than you-- a sure sign of a
>   gentleman. One can tell an awful
>   lot about a man by the erudition
>   with which he speaks.

>   *The SEAMEN glance at each*
>   *other quizzically.*

SEAMAN 2

>   Does that mean if we talk better,
>   we can be capt'ns, too, sir?

CAPTAIN

>   Now you're just being
>   preposterous. Look at me...

>   (*posing & preening*
>   *importantly*)

>   A noble & heroic bearing, with a
>   strong carriage: I was *made* to be
>   a Captain, whilst you sorry lot
>   were made to be sea-dogs. Look at
>   *you*: weak chins, heavy brows... as
>   Mr. Darwin might say, you are
>   (MORE)

CAPTAIN (cont'd)

    adapted to a life of rowing, whereas I am adapted to the difficult job of command.

SEAMAN 3

    I don't know nothin' 'bout Mr. Darwin. Maybe Cap's right: maybe we don't talk good enough to be in charge.

    The CAPTAIN crosses his arms over his chest and looks away smugly. The SEAMEN continue to glance around awkwardly.

SEAMAN 1

    Begging your pardon, Cap, but 'ow long 'ave you been the Cap? I can't recollect your givin' orders nowheres but right 'ere.

SEAMAN 2

    Say, mates, I don't 'member the Cap bein' the Cap, neither. I barely 'member bein' on the ship at all.

SEAMAN 3

    Truth be told, I don't remember nothin' but sittin' in this little tub... seems like days 'n' days now. I can't even remember me own name.

CAPTAIN

> And *that*, crewmen, is why you are crewmen and I'm the Captain.

SEAMAN 1

> Awright, then: what's your name?

CAPTAIN

> Why, my name is... my name is... my name is none of your business, damn your hides!

SEAMAN 2

> Awright, then: what's *my* name?

CAPTAIN

> Your your your your name is none of my business, you you you you lazy dog. Now, let's have an end to this mutinous behavior before we have to resort to courts martial, shall we?

SEAMEN 1, 2, & 3

> (*hastily*)
>
> Yes, sir.

SEAMAN 1

> Say, Cap, if the crew ain't sailed off without us, do you s'pose if we was to wave our arms about 'n' shout we might be able to attract their attention?

CAPTAIN

> (*relieved to have the attention of the SEAMEN diverted elsewhere*)

That's a capital idea! You lot go ahead and start waving, and I'll keep on the lookout for some response. Now, for it, seamen! flap your wings!

> *The SEAMEN begin shouting and waving their arms until their enthusiasm wanes.*

SEAMAN 1

See anything, Cap?

CAPTAIN

Keep waving! I think I see something.

SEAMAN 2

Now, how can ya see aught in this dark? An' there ain't even a light on deck for the night watch.

SEAMAN 3

They're all asleep... in their bunks!

SEAMAN 1

... With a hot meal, and a belly full o' grog!

CAPTAIN

> (*muttering to himself*)

Oh, good god, not again...

> (to the grumbling
>
> SEAMEN)

Well, I remember being in command of our ship, standing at the fo'c'sle, watching the spume race by 'neath us, the scent of the tar softening in the sun, the creak & the groan of the lap-strakes as she hove to, the snap of the sheets...

SEAMAN 1

Beggin' your pardon, sir, but I 'member all that stuff, too.

SEAMAN 2 & 3

Yeah, us, too.

CAPTAIN

> (*defensively*)

Well, then, surely you must remember when I led you ashore?

SEAMAN 2

> (*tentatively*)

Does anyone 'member a storm?

CAPTAIN

> Storm? What storm? Surely if there had been a storm, I should remember it.

SEAMAN 3

> (*more confidently*)
>
> I 'member a storm! 'Twas a howler... indeed it was: as bad as any weather I've seen on the Horn, it was!

CAPTAIN

> There was no storm.

SEAMAN 1

> (*with absolute confidence now*)
>
> Aye, she tossed the old girl for days, she did. Shredded our sheets...

CAPTAIN

> ... No storm.

SEAMAN 2

> ... Shivered me timbers!

CAPTAIN

> (*exasperated*)
>
> *Gentlemen*... and I use the term
>
> (MORE)

CAPTAIN (cont'd)
> loosely... there was no storm, and all this chatter is beginning to look suspiciously like a mutiny. I'm sure no one here wants a court martial... I know *I* don't!

SEAMAN 2
> Say, Cap, if we do 'ave a court martial, an' all three of us is put in the brig... well, just wond'rin', sir, who's gonna row, and where're we gonna put the brig?

SEAMAN 1
> Yeah... it's not like this little walnut shell is brimmin' over with space.

CAPTAIN
>> (*uneasily turning his attention to the distant ship*)
>
> What's that?! Did I hear someone call out?!

SEAMEN 1, 2, & 3
>> (*easily distracted, turning their attention to the ship, waving their arms frantically*)
>
>> (MORE)

SEAMEN 1, 2, & 3 (cont'd)

>Hey! Over here! Hey... somebody... who's on the watch? Hey! Come get us!

>>(*they trail off dispiritedly, muttering*)

SEAMAN 1

>Say, Cap, if you's 'ere with us, who'd'ya s'pose is in command of the ole Missus.?

CAPTAIN

>Don't be ridiculous: the ship's master is in charge of the ship.

SEAMAN 2

>I don't 'member no ship's master, Cap. What if there ain't no ship's master?

>>*The CAPTAIN attempts to reply, but is interrupted.*

SEAMAN 3

>>(*panicky*)

>What if there ain't no crew aboard the ol' girl at'all!? What if they's all like us: stuck on a dory waiting for the rest of the crew t' come rescue 'em?

>   *The CAPTAIN again tries to
>   reply, but is once more
>   interrupted.*

SEAMAN 2

>   Yeah: what if the 'ole crew are
>   just paddlin' 'round 'ere like
>   us... goin' nowheres?

>   *The CAPTAIN is again
>   interrupted.*

SEAMAN 1

>   What we needs is a better plan
>   than what we has.

CAPTAIN

>   Easy, men: You've become deranged!
>   Now, I'm the Captain here...
>   ordained by god and king to command.
>   I'm the man with the plan. You,
>   gentlemen-- and, to reiterate, I use
>   the term loosely-- you are just the
>   crew. Now, let's have no more of
>   this sedition. Let's just stick to
>   *my* plan.

SEAMAN 1

>   Beggin' yer pardon, Cap, but your
>   plan don't seem to be worth a
>   wooden nickel in a house afire.

CAPTAIN

>   (*indignantly*)

>   I am shocked... *shocked*! I have

>   (MORE)

CAPTAIN (cont'd)

> led you men courageously in the face of grave misfortune, and this is how you repay me?! This is blatant insurrection, and I'll not have it on my...

SEAMAN 3

> ... dory? Oh, stow it... *sir*!
>
> (*to SEAMAN 1*)
>
> Right, mate: what's the new plan?

SEAMAN 1

> (*musing*)
>
> Right. Well, first off, let's make me the Cap, eh?
>
> (*The SEAMEN all look at the CAPTAIN, who is attempting to ignore them*)

CAPTAIN

> What?!

SEAMAN 1

> Hand it over, skipper.

CAPTAIN

> Hand it over *sir*. And hand what over, exactly, you perfidious sons of whores?

SEAMAN 1

> Hand over your cap, Cap. It's time you passed the hat.

CAPTAIN

> (*indignantly*)
>
> It takes a lot more than a hat to make a man a Captain!

> > *The SEAMEN continue to wait impatiently, staring at the CAPTAIN, who finally jerks the hat off and, in exasperation, tosses it at SEAMAN 1.*

CAPTAIN

> Fine!'Ere's yer bloody 'at, for whatever that's worth, but you just 'member, it ain't no hat what makes the man!

> > *SEAMAN 1 dons the hat & suddenly affects pomposity.*
> >
> > *SEAMEN 2 & 3 don't notice yet, but are enthusiastic about the change of leadership.*

SEAMAN 2

> Right, then, matey: what's the word?

SEAMAN 3

> What's the new plan, old chum?

SEAMAN 1

> ... *Sir*.

SEAMAN 2

> Sir what?

SEAMAN 1

> Right, then, *sir*, and so forth. Rank does enjoy some privileges. Now, row, you dogs! Row like your lives depend on it! I have no intention of spending even one more day in this little bucket.

SEAMAN 2 & 3

> That's the new plan?!

CAPTAIN

> It feels like day-jah-view all over again, dun' it?

SEAMAN 1

> (musing to himself)

> I'll be a benevolent Captain, one the men will trust in their hour of need, one who inspires them to great acts of heroism.

> (to the crew)

> Row! Row, damn your hides, or I'll take the lash to you! Row... row... row... row...

> *Lights down*

2. The Audition

Based on a Recent Nightmare

Synopsis: A young Assistant Director runs auditions for her demanding, unmannered director for the male lead of a new play. The men who audition are not up to the job, but the quiet janitor has her own ideas.

The Cast:

DIRECTOR: Bobo Maripizi, a late middle-aged Italian-American who speaks like a mafia don; he has a propensity for profanity and a short temper (*this character could also be a woman).

AD: Angela, the assistant director, a young woman just getting started in theatre.

JANITOR: a nameless factotum who cleans the theatre and occasionally helps out with unruly talent (*this character could also be a woman).

ALEXANDER MONTROSE: late 20s- 30s, a small man with an enormous ego, scandal problems, and a bad habit of radically over-acting. A former dancer, he tends to be too physically busy on stage, even when he's not performing, but, he's always performing.

WILLIAM (BILL) LEHMAN: late 20s- 30s, star of stage & screen, Bill is a method actor who can't remember his lines and, as a result, tends to mumble them. When forced to a higher volume, he stutters.

HUNT STEELE: late 20s-30s, a former porn star, Steele has only one character: porn star.

DON O'MALLEY (OS): the tight-fisted producer of the show.

The Stage: An empty theatre.

ACT I

Scene 1

Seated downstage left, the DIRECTOR, wearing a beret & oversized glasses, puffing intermittently on his e-cigarette, & the AD, a nervous youngster juggling a bunch of files, a megaphone, and a brown bag of nuts from which she periodically snacks. Upstage left, the JANITOR is quietly mopping & brooming the floor & wiping down seats. Downstage right is a raised dais with a single fake column against which leans a long, curved sword.

DIRECTOR

>(brusquely, with a strong NY Italian-American accent)

So, what's he say?

AD

He said you can have the Tower, but not the whole Castle.

DIRECTOR

    Cheap mother f....

AD

        (*interrupting, offering her bag of nuts*)

    Filbert? He says you're already over-budget & he wants to see the cast first.

DIRECTOR

        (*repeating*)

    Cheap mother f...

AD

    Filbert?

DIRECTOR

        (*grabs a nut, throws it in his mouth & chews furiously*)

    Alright, who's next?

AD

        (*handing the DIRECTOR a file*)

    This is Alexander Montrose. He...

DIRECTOR

> Montrose? With the woman & the mother & the stolen RV?

AD

> Apparently, the RV was "borrowed", and the woman & her mother settled out of court. He was never charged...

DIRECTOR

> So, what the f...

AD

> Filbert?

DIRECTOR

> ... is he doin' here?

AD

> Well, apparently, he's finished rehab, so his agent's trying to give his career a reboot.

DIRECTOR

> Drunk, dumb f...

AD

> Filbert?

DIRECTOR

> Okay, bring 'im in.

AD

>   (*into a megaphone*)

Alexander Montrose, you're up.

>   *A tiny, over-dressed man, MONTROSE struts onto stage right like a ballet dancer, twirling his body slowly & throwing his arms around dramatically until he ascends the dais.*

MONTROSE

>   (with an exaggerated English accent)

Hello, I... am Alexander Montrose... you know who that is... My agent has a list of my dressing room requirements. I also need a bowl of starburst candies available at all times. I think you'll find that, with Alexander Montrose attached to your project, you'll have a winner.

DIRECTOR

>   Mr. Montrose, why don't we see if you get the part first.

MONTROSE

>Oh, yes, the "formality" of an audition. Very well, then, Alexander Montrose will be reading the second soliloquy, act one, scene one.
>
>>(*MONTROSE picks up the sword & begins twirling & thrusting it*)
>
>For the character of the night watchman I'm channeling the "Rex Harrison" I used for my Tony-nominated Richard Three at the Atlanta Rep.
>
>>(*he turns his back on the DIRECTOR, then spins abruptly, thrusting his sword for emphasis*)
>
>I... met her in the tower... of which I... was a guard on the night watch...

DIRECTOR

>>(*to AD*)
>
>What is this guy, a mutant ninja turtle? Less busy.

AD

> (*into megaphone*)]

Mr. Montrose, a little less movement, please.

> *MONTROSE turns abruptly, whacks the column with the sword, & drops the sword while steadying the column.*

MONTROSE

> (*drops his fake accent for a moment*)

Ooops, sorry.

> (*picking up the sword, he resumes*)

Sorry. Alexander Montrose will be imagining his Stanford Calderwood MacBeth.

> (*clearing his throat, delivers his lines exactly as he did the first time, this time pacing frantically*)

I... met her in the tower... of which I... was a guard on the night watch... duty perilous because the night belongs to... witches...

DIRECTOR

>   Too busy. Too f...

AD

>   Filbert?

DIRECTOR

>   ... busy!

AD

>   >   (*into megaphone*)
>
>   Mr. Montrose, this is a pensive moment for the night watchman: he's ruminating on his personal failings.

MONTROSE

>   Pensive?

AD

>   Thoughtful, meditative.

MONTROSE

>   Ah, I see.
>
>   >   (*adjusting himself*)
>
>   Alexander Montrose will recall his Tanglewood Hamlet.

AD

>   From the top.

MONTROSE

> (*with dramatic flourish, & the exact same delivery*)

I... met...

DIRECTOR

> *Frantically grabbing the megaphone from the AD.*

Next!

MONTROSE

I beg your pardon, sir: you have interrupted Alexander Montrose!

DIRECTOR

Next!

> *The JANITOR gently escorts MONTROSE off stage right.*

MONTROSE

I need a drink. I wonder what Lindsay's up to?

> *MONTROSE exits stage left.*

DIRECTOR

Stupid mother f...

AD

Filbert?

DIRECTOR

>   Who's next?

AD

>   (*handing the DIRECTOR the next file*)

>   William Lehman.

DIRECTOR

>   Do I know this guy? What's he done?

AD

>   (*scanning her own file*)

>   He's got a lot of credits. James Lipton called him "one of the shimmering, magnitude-one stars of the American theatrical constellation". Oh, & Gene Siskel gives him a thumbs-up.

DIRECTOR

>   He's done movies?

AD

>   He's been in all of Michael Bey's movies.

DIRECTOR

>   I don't know who that is. What's the fat guy give 'im?

AD

> The fat guy, sir?

DIRECTOR

> The little fat guy... whatsis... Ebert...

AD

> Oh, um, I guess he doesn't like the way Lehman enunciates.

DIRECTOR

> Thumbs down, huh? Okay, bring 'im in.

AD

> William Lehman, come on in.

>> *A messy, blue-jean & t-shirt clad man with unkempt hair ambles in slouching.*

LEHMAN

> Hi, I'm Bill. Give me just a minute to prepare.

>> *LEHMAN raises his arms & starts making jazz-hands while shaking his face & making strange noises with his mouth.*

DIRECTOR

> (*to the AD*)
>
> What the f...

AD

    Filbert?

DIRECTOR

    ... is with the jazz-hands?

AD

    He's preparing.

DIRECTOR

    Oh, boy. Not another f...

AD

    Filbert?

DIRECTOR

    ... method actor.

        They wait while LEHMAN screams at the ceiling, weeps uncontrollably, and slaps himself across the face.

    Do you suppose he is going to be ready to start any time soon?

AD

        (*into the megaphone*)

    Mr. Lehman, why don't you get started?

LEHMAN

    Just Bill, please. I need to get
        (MORE)

LEHMAN (cont'd)

    inside the character's head. I need to access his pain. Act one, scene one, second soliloquy.

> *LEHMAN gargles and shakes his hands some more, finally spins around, grabs the sword, & sinks to one knee, with his face directed at the floor.*

    Wah mummer nathuh tuhwer, umich wawawawawass agurd ona niwutch, du-ee parlous cuz the nilons blong totototo witches...

DIRECTOR

        (*incredulous*)

    What the f...

AD

    Filbert?

DIRECTOR

    ... is he saying?

        (*to LEHMAN*)

    Mr. Lehman...

LEHMAN

    Just Bill...

DIRECTOR

    Just-Bill, I need to be able to hear the words that are coming out of the hole in your face. My audience needs to be able to hear you. You are not having a private conversation with yourself over here.

LEHMAN

    But he *is* havin' a private conversation with himself, man. He's, like, alone on the hill y'know, with a lonely job, & his buddy Tonto...

AD

    (*interrupting*)

    ... Pontus...

LEHMAN

    ... Pontus, is like blind or a deaf-mute or somethin', man...

DIRECTOR

    And how do you expect my audience to understand all that... telepathy?

LEHMAN

    I don't want the audience to hear

    (MORE)

LEHMAN (cont'd)

>me, man: that's so passé. They need to *feel* me...

DIRECTOR

>Mr. Lehman... Bill, what they are going to be feeling is pissed off that they paid money for tickets to a play that they cannot hear.

LEHMAN

>That's so parochial, man. Sometimes you just have to let the art direct you.

DIRECTOR

>Well, today the director is directing you. Again, from the top.

LEHMAN

>>(*big, dramatic sigh, then, with more volume*)
>
>I met her ininininin the tower, of which I I I I I I was a guard on on on on on on on duty because the the the the the night belongs to bitches...

AD

>...witches...

LEHMAN

>...witches.

DIRECTOR

>Oh, this is painful...

LEHMAN

>...the the the the fearless & cunning, orororor...

DIRECTOR

>Mr. Lehman... Bill, what is with the speech impediment?

LEHMAN

>Oh, that's a technique I use to make the dialog sound more "au naturel".

DIRECTOR

>What about all the other words that were supposed to be in that soliloquy?

LEHMAN

>Well, my technique is good for bridging the lines I drop...

DIRECTOR

>>(*yelling to no one in particular*)
>
>Next! Next! What the f...

AD

    Filbert?

        As LEHMAN is escorted off the dais by the JANITOR, the AD's mobile rings.

DIRECTOR

    Don't answer that.

AD

        (*taking the call*)

    Mr. Maripizi's phone, this is Angela.

        (*pause*)

    Yes, sir, he's right here.

        (*handing the phone to the DIRECTOR*)

    It's Mr. O'Malley.

DIRECTOR

        (*grabbing the phone, becoming very unctuous*)

    Don, how are ya?

        (*pause*)

    We are doing great! We have some first-class talent over here.

        (*pause*)
        (MORE)

DIRECTOR (cont'd)

    Don, Don, Don, I'm tellin' ya, don't worry 'bout it: we got a movie star, we got a Tony winner... what?

        (pause)

    No no no, what?

        (pause)

    They're cheap, Don, cheap...

        (pause)

    Don, don't worry 'bout it: this baby is shaping up great.

        (closed the phone & hands it to the AD)

    Next time it's Don, don't answer. Who's next?

AD

        (handing a file to the DIRECTOR)

    We've got Mr. Hunt Steele.

DIRECTOR

    Hunt Steele? Is that his porn name?

AD

>Yes, sir. He's trying to go mainstream.

DIRECTOR

>>(*incredulous*)
>
>Get the f...

AD

>Filbert?

DIRECTOR

>... outta here.
>
>>(*Looking in the file, scrutinizing a photo up close*)
>
>Holy f...

AD

>Filbert?

DIRECTOR

>Is that anatomically correct? Never mind. Just bring him in.

AD

>>(*into megaphone*)
>
>Mr. Steele, you're up.
>
>>*A beefcake in a shirt from which the sleeves have been*

> *torn and tight spandex pants enters running his fingers compulsively through his hair. He seems very humble and a little diffident as he ascends the dais.*

STEELE

    Hi, my name is Hint Steele... I mean, Hunt, Hunt Steele.

        (he clears his throat nervously)

    I'm sorry, I'm a little nervous. I've never done this with my clothes on before.

AD

    Aw, you'll do fine, Mr. Steele. What are you reading?

STEELE

    Thanks, uh, I'm doin' act one, scene one, soliloquy five... "the prostitutes".

AD

    Okay, whenever you're ready.

STEELE

        (*picking up the sword, stroking it suggestively*)

        (MORE)

STEELE (cont'd)

    Okay, here goes... That is my home, though I am not Greek. My wounds have made me appalling to intimacy...

> (*with his free hand, he tears off his Velcro pants and thrusts his groin*)

    ... so I lay my head among the whores...

> (*he holds the sword at his groin, where it looks disturbingly like an extension of his penis*)

    ... who will touch me for enough gold.

> (*he licks his lips lasciviously*)

DIRECTOR

    What the f...

AD

    Filbert?

STEELE

> (*Caressing his pectorals*)

(MORE)

STEELE (cont'd)

> Who would judge whom in that district, for have we not all sold ourselves one way or another?
>
> > (*grinding his pelvis*)

DIRECTOR

> > (*Grabbing the megaphone again*)
>
> Thank you, Mr. Steele.

STEELE

> Yeah, but I'm not done, yet.

DIRECTOR

> Oh, yes you are. I have seen enough.

STEELE

> *Awesome!*
>
> > (*exits stage right*)
>
> I got the part! I got the part!

DIRECTOR

> Stupid mother f...

AD

> Filbert?

DIRECTOR

>... f...

AD

>Filbert? He's kinda cute, & he did remember all of his lines.

DIRECTOR

>(*to the AD*)
>
>Well, if we ever make an x-rated "Night Watchman", we'll know who to call. Let's take a break. At this rate, we'll never make cast.
>
>>*The DIRECTOR exits stage right; dumping her files, megaphone, & bag on nuts on her chair, the AD hurries after him. Alone on the stage the JANITOR moves tentatively onto the dais and strikes an heroic pose of a stooped & crippled night watchman armed with a mop, delivering his lines beautifully.*

JANITOR

>I met her in the tower, of which I was a guard on the night watch, duty perilous because the night belongs to witches, duty thus reserved for the fearless and the cunning, or maybe only the foolish & the blind. I esteem my self now,
>
>>(MORE)

JANITOR (cont'd)

    looking back over my short life (for I am not aged), having always been foolish; my blindness was a more recent development. They are the same, though-- foolishness & blindness: they permit us the luxury of self-delusion, of believing that what we did mattered, or that what we neglected didn't.

    The JANITOR smiles, bows, & starts mopping the dais.

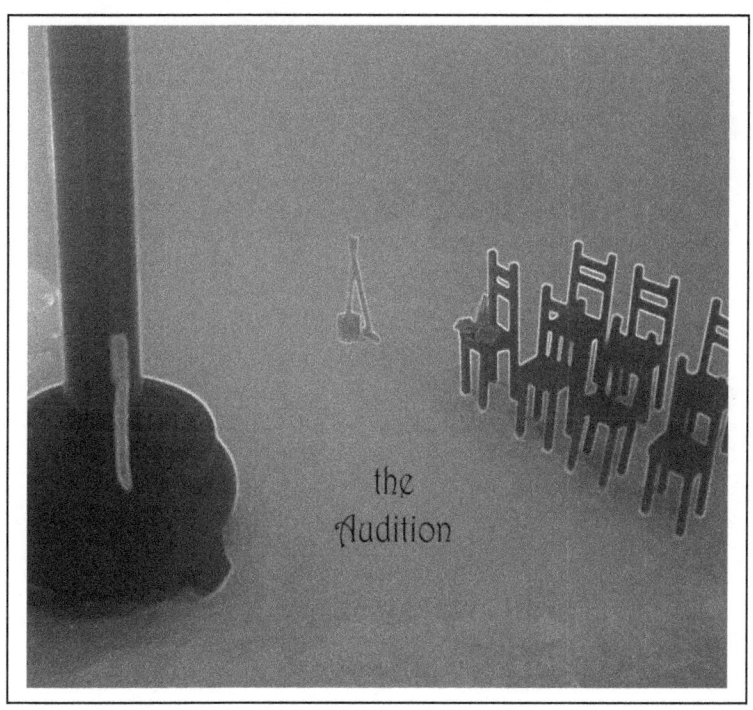

3. Good Grooming

for the Discriminating Gentleman...

Synopsis: Adam has a new problem; Lou Pine has been dealing with it for a while. While the receptionist, Penny, answers the phones, the two men compare notes on life & love as they wait for their monthly grooming at Patty's Puppy Love.

The Cast:

PENNY: a young woman 20s-mid30s, the ultra-compassionate receptionist at the beauty salon "Penny's Puppy Love".

ADAM PUSTLNKRER: a young, gay man 20s-30s, a novice coming to the beauty salon for the first time, a little apprehensive about his circumstances.

LOU PINE: a mature man late 30s-40s, a refined, masculine metrosexual with some life experience.

PATTY: a woman, the owner of "Patty's Puppy Love".

The Stage: The waiting room at Patty's Puppy Love.

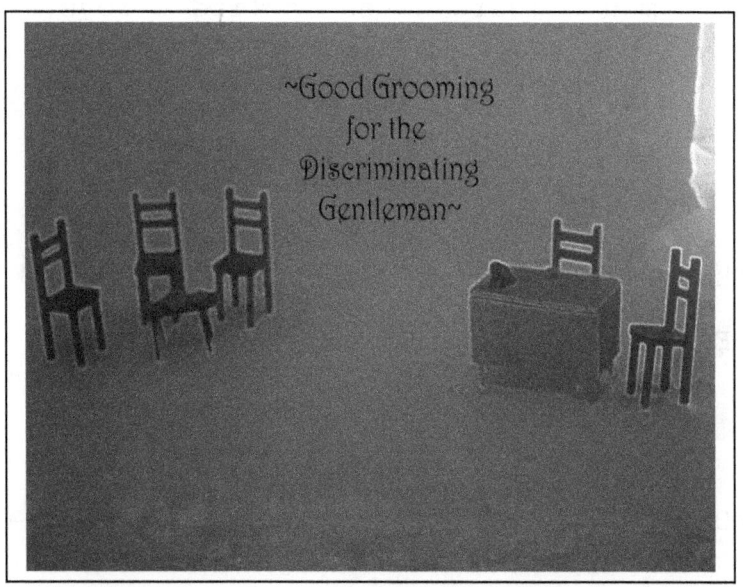

ACT I

Scene 1

Downstage right, a low table with a few magazines, & a few chairs, one of which is occupied by LOU PINE, who is reading a magazine. Downstage left, a simple desk with a phone, an appointment book, some clipboards, & a few photo albums. PENNY sits behind the desk minding her nails. An empty chair faces her on the side of her desk. PENNY answers the phone.

PENNY

    Thank you for calling Patty's Puppy Love. My name is Penny. How can I help you today?

        (*pause, listening to reply.*)

PENNY

    Yes, sir, we are a full-service
        (MORE)

PENNY (cont'd)

Groomer.

(*pause*)

At PPL we like to customize our grooming services to the individual needs of our clients, so we might only do a basic shampoo, cut, & dry, or we might provide "the works", which also includes teeth cleaning & claw trimming. What do you think you might be interested in?

(*pause, flipping through the appointment book*)

Well, we're booked pretty heavily for the next week— full moon, y'know— but I do have an opening next Tuesday morning at 10.

(*pause*)

I'll call you if I get a cancelation between now & then.

PENNY pauses, writing in the appointment book. ADAM PUSTLNKRER enters stage left & stops at the desk. PENNY gives him a little wave. He waits while she finishes with her call.

(MORE)

PENNY (cont'd)
> Mr. Barker... B- A- R- K- E- R-- well, isn't that a nice name. Okay, we'll see ya then. Plan on coming in a few minutes early so we can fill out your client questionnaire and look through our style book.
>
> *PENNY hangs up and addresses ADAM.*

PENNY
> 'Morning.
>
> *ADAM mumbles a response PENNY can't hear.*
>
> I'm sorry, sir?
>
> *ADAM clears his throat nervously & tries a little louder.*

ADAM
> Hmmmp hmmp hmm. Sorry. I think I have an appointment with you.
>
> *PENNY glances at her appointment book.*

PENNY
> Let's see. Mr. Pus... stil... nik... ker... rer?

ADAM

    It's eastern European. You can call me Adam. That's me. Are you Patty?

PENNY

    Oh, no, Patty's my boss. My name's Penny. Why don't you sit & we'll work on your client questionnaire?

> *ADAM takes a seat beside the desk. PENNY picks up one of the clip boards & extracts a pen from her hair.*

ADAM

    (*fidgeting*)

    I'm a little nervous. I've never done anything like this before.

PENNY

    Awwww. Don't worry. We're gonna make this a wonderful experience for you. I promise you'll have fun. Okay, so, how did you hear about PPL?

ADAM

    A friend at the dog park mentioned you.

PENNY

    Ever been to a beauty salon before-- nope: already answered that one. Okay, married or single?

ADAM

>Married... sort of... in 17 states & the District of Columbia...

PENNY

>Name of spouse?

ADAM

>Adore... Steve Adore...

PENNY

>Awww, Adam & Steve... sweet. How long have you been married... sort of?

ADAM

>We sort-of married two years ago, but we've been together for twelve.

PENNY

>Awww... how romantic.

ADAM

>Aren't you gonna write that down?

PENNY

>Oh, no: that's not on the questionnaire. I was just bein' nosy. Occupation?

ADAM

>Steve's?

PENNY

> Well, sure, why not?

ADAM

> He's a manager at Banana Republic... you're not writing that down, either.

PENNY

> Nope.

ADAM

> Mine?

PENNY

> Umhum.

ADAM

> I'm a hair dresser.

PENNY

> Awww... see: you make people beautiful; now it's our turn to make you beautiful. How long have you had your condition?

ADAM

> Two years. We were on vacation in London...

PENNY

> We get that a lot... you'd be

(MORE)

PENNY (cont'd)

> surprised. Adam, what are your expectations for you visit with us today?

ADAM

> Oh, I don't know. I guess I just feel like it's time I started taking care of myself a little. If I don't owe it to myself, I at least owe it to Steve not to let myself go completely.

PENNY

> Is there any particular concern you'd like us to address today?

ADAM

> Steve says I have an odor, especially when it rains. I smell whenever it rains.

PENNY

> Yeah, we hear that a lot, too.

>> *ADAM scratches at himself furiously; PENNY pulls away a little.*

ADAM

> It's not fleas. The allergist says I have dry skin.

PENNY

>	I think we can help with that, too. We can recommend some supplements that'll clear that right up. Okay, last question: what do you want to leave here with today?

ADAM

>	Oh, I don't know. I want something cute, you know... playful...

PENNY

>	Teeth & claws?

ADAM

>	Sure, why not?

>	*PENNY opens one of the albums.*

PENNY

>	Okay, so this is our basic style book. The tabs are colour-coded for easy reference. The pink section is "just adorable", but maybe just glance through the rest of the book: black is "goth-biker", blue is "seriously you, GQ", red is "glamour", yellow is "around the house", & green is "upscale pampered". You can mix-and-match, too, so if you see something you want to add to the

(MORE)

PENNY (cont'd)
> "cute" design, we can customize it for you. & this is our waiver & disclosure for teeth & nails. Just fill in the blanks, date & sign it. Why don't you take a seat in the waiting room, & I'll call you when we're ready.
>
> *PENNY hands ADAM the album & clip board. He moves to a vacant seat beside LOU PINE & starts filling out the form. LOU PINE quietly intrudes*

LOU
> Doggie smell, huh?

ADAM
> (*shrugging*)
>
> I wash & wash...

LOU
> Beginner's mistake. Don't sweat it. I'm Lou... Lou Pine.

ADAM
> Adam Pustlnkrer.

LOU
> Yeah, I Heard. That's a doozy.

ADAM

> It's Eastern European... no vowels... You can call me Adam.

LOU

> Adam, nice to meet you.

ADAM

> I've never done anything like this before.

LOU

> I heard that. It's a step. You have a lot to learn about living with your condition. I remember when I was first bit...

ADAM

> Where was that?

LOU

> On my hand.

ADAM

> No, I mean, where were you when you got bit?

LOU

> I was on business in Romania.

ADAM

> Ooh, Romania! I hear it's beautiful!

LOU

> Yeah, very old-world... very agrarian... and they love people from the states. Very spooky, though: you can't swing a dead rat without hitting some kind of monster. You don't see that in the U.S.-- our monsters are all just lawyers & bankers.

ADAM

> What do you do?

LOU

> I'm a lawyer... for a big bank. That's why I was in Romania-- taking care of business. After that, it wasn't a tough choice: blood-sucking vampire or wolf-in-sheep's-clothing. I was in Bucharest for my first moon, & I accidentally urinated on the couches in the lobby a couple of times. When housekeeping showed up at my door with pitchforks & torches, I knew right away this was gonna be no picnic. What's your story?

ADAM

> Oh, I don't really have a story...

LOU

    Come one, bother: we all have a story. How'd you end up here?

ADAM

    Well, we were on vacation in London-- it was sort of our honeymoon-- and ran into another American. Normally Steve & I don't swing, but he was just so cute...

LOU

    What happened?

ADAM

    He was a biter, turned out.

LOU

    What happened to your husband?

ADAM

    Oh, nothing-- he remembered the safe-word. I forgot.

> (*awkward moment of silence*)

    It was "stay".

LOU

    You couldn't remember "stay"? Not that I'm judging...

ADAM

>Well, it's easy to remember now!

>>*ADAM scratches furiously again, adds sheepishly)*

>Dry skin.

LOU

>Olive oil.

ADAM

>Rub it on?

LOU

>Cook with it, drink it. More is better.

>>*The phone rings; PENNY takes the call.*

PENNY

>Thank you for calling Patty's Puppy Love. My name is Penny. How can I help you today?

>>(*pause*)

>Yes, we do.

>>(*pause*)

>The standard toe-nail trim is $50.00; the deluxe toe-nail dremmelization is $100.00. If you have unnaturally long quicks, or
>>(MORE)

PENNY (cont'd)

    if you haven't had your nails trimmed before, I recommend the dremmelization-it takes a little longer, but there's much less bleeding.

        (*Pause*)

    You have to sign the standard waiver & release indemnifying PPL against accidental pain & suffering.

ADAM

    Steve says that my claws hurt in bed.

LOU

    My girlfriend likes them just sharp enough to leave marks, but not so sharp they draw blood.

ADAM

    She knows about your...

LOU

    She's been great-- very accepting. She's really helped me get in touch with my feminine side. I have to admit, I like a nice hair style, & the mani/pedi here is heaven. There was this Vietnamese

        (MORE)

LOU (cont'd)

>girl-- Hue-- she could literally curl my toes.

ADAM

>I'm gettin' the mani/pedi. Should I ask for her?

LOU

>No, she's gone-- workman's compensation. The new girl's good, though.
>
>>(*Pause*)
>
>She smells like lamb...

ADAM & LOU

>>(*in a reverie*)
>
>Mmmmmmmm...

LOU

>Hey, have you been to the new carpaccio place on Central Ave? You've gotta try it: it's... like... seven different kinds of meat, fowl, & fish, with a fig reduction and a lovely little Kalamata tapenade...

ADAM

>Ooh, you know who else's got great meat is Braza Leña-- they bring it
>>(MORE)

ADAM (cont'd)

right to your table rare & still smoking on a steel skewer... although they're a little uncooperative in the doggie-bag department.

ADAM & LOU

Mmmmmm...

ADAM

How long have you had your moon?

LOU

It'll be five years next month. The first couple of years were pretty tough. First it seemed like a big old party-- chasing girls, running amok, the crazy night life-- but then I would go to the park to play Frisbee with my bros, & I kept wanting to catch it in my teeth. And the car-chasing thing-- that was a little embarrassing. Tennis was completely out of the question, and the postman wasn't exactly a big fan. Plus...

(*LOU leans close to ADAM*)

... I had this weird thing with cat poop.

ADAM

>	I know!

LOU

>	What is that about?!

ADAM

>	OMG, I was like, "Mrs. Wiener"-- she's our neighbor-she's got like twenty-five cats... well, twenty-three now-- "Mrs. Wiener, would you like me to clean your yard?" Cat poop under every geranium... and the petunias were a gold mine! Have you noticed that wealthy people have better tasting cat poop?

LOU

>	It's the diet, man: Friskies in, Friskies out; sautéed salmon fillets with capers in, sautéed salmon fillets with capers out...

ADAM

>	I haven't mentioned this to Steve...

LOU

>	Yeah, maybe don't. I'm not advocating keeping secrets from your partner, but...

ADAM

>TMI?

LOU

>Way too...

ADAM

>>(*nodding*)
>
>Beginner's mistake.

LOU

>Here's a little trick for ya: keep some good bonbons in the freezer. They'll help ya over the rough patches.
>
>>*The phone rings again; PENNY takes the call.*

PENNY

>Thank you for calling Patty's Puppy Love. My name is Penny. How can I help you today?
>
>>(*pause*)
>
>All of our technicians are certified at the Warren Zevon Institute of Discrete Grooming Sciences.
>
>>(*Pause*)
>
>Have you ever had a professional
>
>>(MORE)

PENNY (cont'd)

    grooming before?

        (*Pause*)

    Ever been to a massage parlour?

        (*Pause*)

    Kinda like that, only with grooming...

        (*Pause*)

    Sorry?

        (*Pause*)

    No, I'm sorry, we don't offer the happy ending...

        (*Pause*)

    Hello? Hello?

LOU

    I'll tell ya one thing: the sex has never been better! No more little blue pills, no more internet porn: the moon comes up, and away we go!

ADAM

    My Steve's a little worried about the mixed marriage thing.

LOU

    Does he want to turn?

ADAM

> I won't let him. One scary beast in the family's enough, don't you think?

LOU

> That's what my girlfriend says. When she moved in, it was like nag-nag-nag-nag, you know: "honey, throw out your damned beer bottles, and stop clawing the furniture". Then I realized she was just trying to help me better myself.

ADAM

> She seems pretty progressive...

LOU

> Yeah, you have no idea. I'm a lucky guy. My ex- was a cat person; boy, did that not work out! Things are great now. Sometimes my gf & I will play dress-up: I'll put on the night cap & gown, and she'll put on her little red riding hood... she carries a basket of goodies...
>
> > *ADAM cocks his head quizzically.*
>
> ... I guess you had to be there...

ADAM

>   (*Aside*)
>
> And people think we're kinky...

LOU

> Hey, I'm not gonna tell you what to do, but you can't make a decision like this for your guy.

ADAM

> We're seeing a marriage counselor-- my rabbi, actually. Steve says he feels like I'm always ready to bite his head off.
>
>   *The phone rings again; PENNY takes the call.*

PENNY

> Thank you for calling Patty's Puppy Love. My name is Penny. How can I help you today?
>
>   (*Pause*)
>
> Oh, hello, Mr. Rottweiler. They just faxed us the court order this morning.
>
>   (*Pause*)
>
> I've scheduled your emergency tooth extraction for tomorrow at 9.
>
>   (MORE)

PENNY (cont'd)

> (pause)
>
> Just the four canines... awww, don't cry, Mr. Rottweiler. Trust me, we'll take good care of you... Awwww.

LOU

> (*Shaking his head*)
>
> Biter. Not cool. If he doesn't get the extraction, they'll put him down. Harsh.

ADAM

> (*Shocked*)
>
> Who'll put 'im down?!

LOU

> The ASPCW.

ADAM

> (*Looks puzzled*)
>
> The what?

LOU

> American Society for the Prevention of Cruelty to... well, you know...

ADAM

> Geez... that seems a little extreme.

LOU

>No, we're lucky: bad apple, et cetera.

ADAM

>>(*Still studying the photo album, holds a photo up for LOU to see*)
>
>I think I want the poodle cut, but I'm so nervous. I wish Steve were here. Do you think I'm making a mistake?

LOU

>I don't know: I think you'll be a good lookin' guy in a poodle cut & a turtle neck. Plus, if you don't like it, you can always change it next month.

ADAM

>What are you getting?

LOU

>>(*taking the book, opens to another page*)
>
>Here, I'm going for the classic Lon Chaney, with maybe a little off the sides-- still masculine, but sensitive. It never gets old.

ADAM

> That's why they call it a classic. Claws & teeth?

LOU

> Oh, yeah: when I come here, I go for the works. I've got the cash, & I think I'm worth it.

ADAM

> That's what my mom's always telling me. Say, what did your parents think?

LOU

> I haven't told them. My mom's pretty conservative.

ADAM

> Oh, no: give her a chance. She just might surprise you. You can't live your life in the closet. After my pink hair phase, and the cross-dressing experimentation, and then bringing home Steve, my mom thought this whole thing was a breeze. Of course, she still doesn't want me at the trailer park when I'm in my moon.

LOU

> I hear ya, brother.

ADAM

> Say, I'm really new at this, and I feel like you've kinda got a few things figured out. Are there any more tips I should know? You know-- I'd like to skip over the rest of the beginner's mistakes...

LOU

> No, you're doin' it, man: it doesn't matter how wild you get: nothin' says "Hey, I'm civilized" like a good grooming.

>> *PATTY enters stage right, in red bandages.*

PATTY

> Mr. Pine, we're ready for you now.

>> *Close curtains.*

4. The Commencement Speaker

Synopsis: globetrotting philanthropist Frank N. Stein-Monster delivers the commencement address at Harkley University, with a little help from his old friend, Igor.

The Cast:

FRANK N. STEIN-MONSTER: the globetrotting philanthropist & philosopher, and product of the experiments of mad scientist Viktor Frankenstein.

IGOR: the slouching, fawning former lab technician, close personal friend, & translator of Dr. Stein-Monster.

THE DEAN: The CEO of Harkley
    University.

The Stage: the stage at the Harkley
    University graduation.

ACT I

Scene 1

Downstage center is a lectern. downstage right, three seated people dressed in formal attire, DR. FRANK N. STEIN-MONSTER, a giant man with green skin, IGOR, a small & hunched man, & THE DEAN, quite ordinary. *optional: downstage left are 6 or 8 chairs occupied by people randomly selected from the audience, facing the lectern.

THE DEAN

      (*rising, taking the podium*)

Good evening, students, faculty, friends, & family of the graduating class of 2018 Harkley University. We are very pleased to

      (MORE)

THE DEAN (cont'd)

> have as our special guest today someone very well known to you. CEO of the 1313-Mockingbird-Lane-Group, polar explorer, concert violinist, poet, & scholar, he has been a leader in combatting prejudice against vampires, werewolves, zombies, and other differently-abled people around the world. Ladies & gentlemen, please give an enthusiastic welcome to DR. FRANK N. STEIN-MONSTER.

>> *Applause. THE DEAN sits; STEIN-MONSTER takes the podium; IGOR assumes a position slightly to his right & downstage.*

IGOR

>> (*to the audience*)

> We are so pleased to be here-- thank you so very much for inviting us to speak to you today. My name is Igor, & I will be translating for Dr. Stein-Monster this evening.

>> (*IGOR defers to STEIN-MONSTER*)

STEIN-MONSTER

> (*Grunting, gesticulating with hands & arms*)

Grrrrrr... grrrr... grrgrrrrr...

> (*and so on...*)

IGOR

> I look across a sea of youthful faces...

STEIN-MONSTER

> Grrrr...

IGOR

> ...so innocent & pure, except for the ones who were in Florida or Mexico on spring break... & the girls-gone-wild... & the frat boys...

STEIN-MONSTER

> Grrr...

IGOR

> I see a tribe of pupae waiting to turn into magnificent butterflies & embark on their next adventure, soaring fearlessly into the wide world... And what a world it is!

STEIN-MONSTER

> Grrrrr...

IGOR

> Times have changed. Whereas once we were defined by the class into which we were born... or revivified... today, in this country, you can become anyone you want to be, anyone you can imagine...

STEIN-MONSTER

> Grrrrr....

IGOR

> Today you graduate from one of the most prestigious universities in the country, prepared to achieve greatness. I'm not as smart as any of you-- my brain came out of the skull of a criminal!-- and yet I have been able to achieve some small measure of greatness: I am not limited by the deficits of my body-parts. 200 years ago, I was just a dumb cadaver, lurching around the lab, snoozing on the slab; today I own that lab... that slab, the vat where I was born...

STEIN-MONSTER

    Grrrr...

IGOR

    More than any time before, society is learning to embrace diversity. Adam can marry Steve; Angela can marry Eve. Black skin, brown, red, yellow, even green--no problem: we have become a rainbow of humanity. To paraphrase Dr. King-- who, as I understand it, was *not* a mad scientist-- we are judged by the quality of our character rather than the colour of our skin.

STEIN-MONSTER

    Grrrr...

IGOR

    When I first escaped from the castle, the only friend I had was a blind old man with a violin. The peasants hated me because I was different: they greeted that difference as an angry mob. Today we celebrate difference: we are more than the sum of our parts: we are each unique, just like everybody else.

STEIN-MONSTER

>	Grrr...

IGOR

>	When I came to this country I had no skills, almost no English, and just the clothes on my back, but through hard work & the relentless pursuit of knowledge I raised myself up: today I am a respected businessman who owns nice clothes & speaks...
>
>>	(*pauses, glances at STEIN-MONSTER*)

STEIN-MONSTER

>	Grrr...

IGOR

>>	(*hesitantly*)
>
>	... speaks English...
>
>>	(*pauses, glances again at STEIN-MONSTER*)

STEIN-MONSTER

>>	(*assertively*)
>
>	Grrr...

IGOR

> (*shrugging with resignation*)

... speaks English perfectly...

STEIN-MONSTER

Grrrr...

IGOR

I have led a life of great good fortune. I am grateful every day to my maker for... well, you know. Like me, he made the pursuit of knowledge the foundation of his life. Maybe he could have been a little neater with the sutures-- he was a little less detail-oriented than he could have been.

STEIN-MONSTER

> (*angry*)

Grrr...

IGOR

I'm a little resentful of that, I guess. He was a surgeon, for heaven's sake: he couldn't sew better than this? Jeez, hire a seamstress... But it's okay: I'm not going to hold a grudge...

STEIN-MONSTER

> Grrr...

IGOR

> I'm grateful for Mrs. Stein-Monster... well, mostly grateful... It's important to have a companion as we go through this life... I love my wife, yes, I do...

STEIN-MONSTER

> Grrr...

IGOR

> Okay, honestly, he could have made me any bride he wanted, and he makes me someone who looks like Elsa Lanchester? I couldn't have someone who looks more like a Kardashian? What's that: mad scientist humour?! I mean, come on... but it's okay: I love my wife...

STEIN-MONSTER

> Grrr...

IGOR

> If I were complaining, I'd
>> (MORE)

IGOR (cont'd)

complain about the fact that I can't go to the beach. I get tan lines... GREEN tan lines... unless I wear a onesie-- yeah, what a fashion-plate! The paba-free SPF2000 makes my sutures itch! My neck bolts rust in the sea water! The only happy part of going to the beach is that I usually have the place to myself!

(*glances at STEIN-MONSTER*)

Eh, please excuse me a moment.

IGOR whispers briefly with STEIN-MONSTER, during which their conversation becomes quite heated. After a few moments, he resumes facing the audience.

STEIN-MONSTER

(calmer again)

Grrr...

IGOR

But I digress. I have lived a rich, full life, and if I would

(MORE)

IGOR (cont'd)

> have you leave here with a sample of my philosophies for living, it would be these points:

STEIN-MONSTER

> Grrrr...

IGOR

> Take care of your body: a good work-out regimen is the key to combatting rigor mortis.

STEIN-MONSTER

> Grrr...

IGOR

> Be self-aware: the left hand should always know what the right hand is doing, especially if they come from different cadavers.

STEIN-MONSTER

> Grrr...

IGOR

> Have the courage of your convictions: the peasants may chase you with pitchforks & torches, but they can only kill
> (MORE)

IGOR (cont'd)

you once, unless you've got a reasonably competent doctor.

STEIN-MONSTER

Grr...

IGOR

Find someone to love: you'll know she's the one... or he, he could be the one... Not for me, but, I mean, if you go that way... or if you're a girl... unless you do go that way, in which case... oh, just find someone to love. You'll know you've found the one when the sparks fly.

STEIN-MONSTER

Grrr...

IGOR

Which brings up my last point: even the darkest cloud has a silver lining, and on a really good day the occasional lightning bolt. Thank you, good luck, & good night.

Lights out.

5. Contraïndications

Synopsis: A thrill-seeking blind woman making photographs of a rattlesnake encounters an herpetologist who's afraid of snakes, & everything else. Together they explore what it really means to be blind & to be afraid.

The Cast:

The WOMAN: an adventurous, blind photographer.

The HERPETOLOGIST: a phobic fellow who studies reptiles, amphibians, & other terrifying things.

The Stage: A forest clearing with a
    picnic table in the back ground.

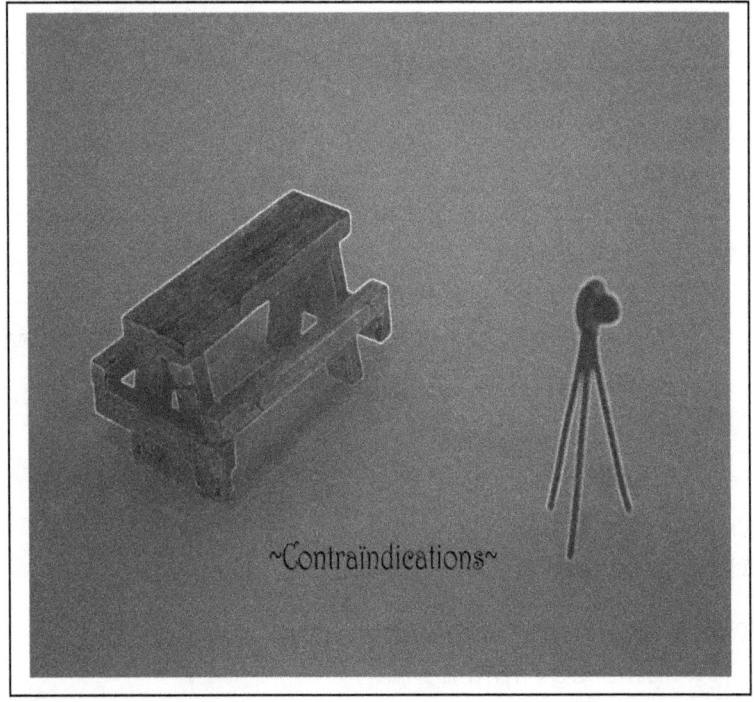
~Contraindications~

Act 1

Scene I

Enter the WOMAN with a 35mm camera on a tripod over one shoulder, and in her other hand a seeing-eye stick with which she is probing the path before her. Hearing a faint hissing & rattling, she pauses & scans her surrounds with her ears & nose.

The WOMAN

   There you are!

She opens the tripod and begins to aim the camera in the direction toward which she was listening & sniffing.

Enter the HERPETOLOGIST, brandishing a snake hook, staring intently at the

> *ground as he walks. Thus distracted, he stumbles into the WOMAN, who is likewise distracted by her camera; his safari hat & snake hook, and her cane, fall to the ground in a tangle.*

The HERPETOLOGIST

    Ooops—sorry: I didn't see you.

The WOMAN

> (*brusquely*)

    That's supposed to be *my* excuse.

The HERPETOLOGIST

    Sorry... I got distracted.

> *The HERPETOLOGIST picks up the cane, the stick, & the hat. He tries to hand her the cane, but drops it on the ground in front of her.*

The WOMAN

    By what?

The HERPETOLOGIST

    Oh, lots of things. Right now, I'm looking for snakes. I'm an herpetologist.

> *The HERPETOLOGIST picks up the cane again and waves his hand in front of the WOMAN's eyes.*

The HERPETOLOGIST

    I study...

The WOMAN & the HERPETOLOGIST

        (*simultaneously*)

    ... reptiles & amphibians.

The HERPETOLOGIST

    You know! Most people don't know that. Most people think it's about STDs.

The WOMAN

    Really? Why?

The HERPETOLOGIST

    Why? What...? Well, because it sounds like... well...

The WOMAN

    ... Well, I'm not *most people*.

> *The HERPETOLOGIST waves his hand in front of the WOMAN's eyes again and eyes the*

    (MORE)

The WOMAN (cont'd)

> *camera suspiciously.*

Stop that!

> *The HERPETOLOGIST is chagrined & recoils a bit, studying the WOMAN, who continues aiming her camera.*

The HERPETOLOGIST

What're ya doin'?

The WOMAN

Making photographs.

The HERPETOLOGIST

(quizzically)

Really? Great! That's great. That's nice. Wow... making... photographs... wow...

(*abruptly*)

Aren't you blind?

> *The WOMAN focuses her ears and presses the trigger on the camera.*

The WOMAN

Umhum.

The HERPETOLOGIST

    Uh, I don't mean to be rude, but...

        (*pauses*)

The WOMAN

    But what?

The HERPETLOGIST

    Well, but... don't you see an essential contradiction here?

The WOMAN

    Where?

The HERPETOLOGIST

    Here... you know... I mean, you're blind.

The WOMAN

    Yeah?

The HERPETOLOGIST

    ... and making photos...

The WOMAN

    Umhum.

The HERPETOLOGIST

    ... and you're blind & making photos...

The WOMAN

> Umhum.

The HERPETOLOGIST

> ... and that's *not* a contradiction?

The WOMAN

> I don't know: is it?

The HERPETOLOGIST

>> (*snorting*)
>
> Well, what kind of photos can you possibly make if you can't see?!

The WOMAN

> I make photos of the way things smell, the way things sound and feel...

The HERPETOLOGIST

>> (*feigning an epiphany*)
>
> Ahhhh...
>
>> (*then, abruptly*)
>
> *That's nuts!*

The WOMAN

> Really?

The HERPETOLOGIST

>   Well, yeah! How do you make a
>   photo of a smell?!
>
>   > *The WOMAN turns the camera so
>   > the HERPETOLOGIST can see the
>   > screen and presses a few
>   > buttons.*

The WOMAN

>   Look: what do you see?

The HERPETOLOGIST

>   Hmmm... It looks like a sunset...
>   a red & gold sunset, with a dark
>   blue ocean & a dark blue sky...
>   the colours are very vibrant...

The WOMAN

>   Is there a flower?

The HERPETOLOGIST

>   Yeah, a cluster of tiny white
>   flowers.

The WOMAN

>   That's what jasmine smells like at
>   dusk.

The HERPETOLOGIST

>   Oh...

The WOMAN

>   (*presses another button*)
>
> What do you see now?

The HERPETOLOGIST

> Ah... uhh... everything's a sort of steely grey... there are all these shiny glass balls floating in the air...

The WOMAN

> Are the balls exploding?

The HERPETOLOGIST

> I don't... yeah, I guess... yeah, they are.

The WOMAN

> That's what rain feels like when it's hitting my skin.

The HERPETOLOGIST

> Hmmm...

The WOMAN

>   (*presses another button*)
>
> What'd'ya see now?

The HERPETOLOGIST

> There's a tree on a hill... a tree-trunk, really, with a few big branches... and then all around it a big smudge of swirly green & yellow stuff...

The WOMAN

> That's the sound of the wind in the leaves.

The HERPETOLOGIST

> (*incredulous, but impressed*)
>
> I'll be darned. You really aren't *most people*. So, what're ya shooting now?

The WOMAN

> Here, look: you'll especially like this one.
>
> > *The WOMAN redirects the camera at her original target; the HERPETOLOGIST peers through the lens. A faint hiss is heard of stage, & a rattle. The HERPETOLOGIST screams, leaps into the air, and bounds up onto a nearby picnic table.*

The HERPETOLOGIST

   Run! Run!

The WOMAN

         (*glancing left & right, alarmed*)

   What?! What's wrong?!

The HERPETOLOGIST

   Run! There's a snake! Run!

The WOMAN

         (*exasperated, resuming her work*)

   I know there's a snake! I'm photographing what it sounds like when it hisses & rattles.

The HERPETOLOGIST

   That's *nuts*!

The WOMAN

   Would you stop saying that!

      She hears the snake rattle & hiss again.

   Ah, there you are. Just ignore him.

         (*to the HERPETOLOGIST*)
         (MORE)

The WOMAN (cont'd)

I can't believe you're afraid of a little snake!

The HERPETOLOGIST

Hello! It's a deadly animal!

The WOMAN

And you call yourself a herpetologist?

The HERPETOLOGIST

I *am* an herpetologist!

The WOMAN

I don't mean to be rude, but, *essential contradictions* and all that?

The HERPETOLOGIST

(*genuinely puzzled*)

What'd'ya mean?

The WOMAN

It's a snake...

The HERPETOLOGIST

So?

The WOMAN

... And you're a herpetologist...

The HERPETOLOGIST

    What'd'ya mean?

The WOMAN

    I suppose I'm just curious how it is a man afraid of snakes ends up studying them.

The HERPETOLOGIST

    Turns out I always end up studying the things I'm afraid of.

The WOMAN

    How Freudian of you.

The HERPETOLOGIST

    Snakes are my life.

        (*in a dreamy voice*)

    Crotalus adamanteus: so lean, so beautiful, so quick. Their skin is so complex: each tiny scale a plate of armour, all the scales together a tapestry, and every once in a while the snake crawls out of its skin and gets to start all over again, like it's brand new.

        The snake rattles again; the HERPETOLOGIST shrieks in
        (MORE)

The HERPETOLOGIST (cont'd)

terror.

Snake! Run! Jeez-Louise: that thing's gonna give me a heart attack!

The WOMAN resumes working the camera, pausing to listen between adjustments.

Watch it! Watch it! What if it lunges?!

The WOMAN

Shhhhhh. This one's a beauty.

The HERPETOLOGIST

What... huh? How can you tell?

The WOMAN

Shhh: just listen. See how deep her voice is when she hisses—how full and round her body must be? And that rattle: that sounds like a *big* rattle. She must be an old snake.

The HERPETOLOGIST

(*leaning closer from his tabletop refuge*)

How old, d'ya think?

The WOMAN

> You tell me—you're the expert.

The HERPETOLOGIST

> Well, I can't see it from way up here, now, can I?

The WOMAN

> *Way up here*? What did you do, climb a tree?

The HERPETOLOGIST

> Ha-ha. Very funny.

>> *The HERPETOLOGIST steps off the table & peers cautiously past the WOMAN.*

> My god! That thing's huge!

>> *The snake rattles again; the HERPETOLOGIST retreats reflexively to the bench of the table.*

The WOMAN

> What else are you afraid of?

The HERPETOLOGIST

> Oh, the usual things: spiders, scorpions, bats, rats, peanut butter sticking to the roof of my mouth...

The WOMAN

> *Peanut butter?!* I guess it's a good thing you don't study peanuts...

The HERPETOLOGIST

> Phew! I'll say! Just the thought of it—ooooooooooo!
>
> (*shivering*)
>
> What are you afraid of?

The WOMAN

> Nothing.

The HERPETOLOGIST

> Aw, c'mon. you must be afraid of something.

The WOMAN

> Like what?

The HERPETOLOGIST

> Like... well... dust balls. I'm terrified of dust balls!

The WOMAN

> Just sweep them up.

The HERPETOLOGIST

> A wall of green paint!

The WOMAN

    Paint the wall red.

The HERPETOLOGIST

    I don't like red paint.

The WOMAN

    So, panel it.

The HERPETOLOGIST

    Oh, good god, no! Too much like the woods.

The WOMAN

    We're *in* the woods.

The HERPETOLOGIST

    Yechhh. Camping & tents & sleepovers...

        (*shivering again*)

The WOMAN

    Yeah, I don't like sleepovers, either.

The HERPETOLOGIST

    Hah! So, you are afraid of something: you're afraid of relationships!

The WOMAN

> No! Well, maybe. Nah. Look, even if there is something I'm afraid of, why would I want to talk about it?

The HERPETOLOGIST

> I don't know... it's like comparing tv shows or prescriptions. Hey, what kinds of meds are you on? I have seven different prescriptions... I'm kinda afraid of being happy.

The WOMAN

> Now *that's* nuts!
>
> > (*distracted by the camera*)
>
> Come here. Take a look at this.
>
> > *Timidly the HERPETOLOGIST creeps down from the bench and looks into the camera. Sniffing the air, he turns his head slightly to look at the WOMAN.*
>
> What is it?

The HERPETOLOGIST

> What is what?

The WOMAN

>Whatever it is you're smelling?

The HERPETOLOGIST

>Well, uhhh, *you,* actually. You smell beautiful. Is that a perfume?

>>*The WOMAN retreats slightly from the HERPETOLOGIST.*

The WOMAN

>I don't wear perfume.

The HERPETOLOGIST

>Oh, thank goodness. I'm afraid of perfume, but you smell so...

The WOMAN

>What'd'ya think of the photo?

The HERPETOLOGIST

>Wow! You're good! This is really beautiful. What is it... I mean, aside from the obvious?

The WOMAN

>It's the sound of a rattle snake rattling.

>>*The snake rattles again; the*
>>(MORE)

>   *HERPETOLOGIST squeaks &*
>   *springs back onto the bench;*
>   *the WOMAN makes the photo.*

The WOMAN

   Gotchya!

The HERPETOLOGIST

       (*screaming*)

   Mother of god!

>   *The snake rattles again; the*
>   *HERPETOLOGIST leaps onto the*
>   *tabletop; the WOMAN makes*
>   *another photo. The*
>   *HERPETOLOGIST is panting,*
>   *swatting and clawing at the*
>   *air.*

   Maybe I should have studied peanuts.

The WOMAN

   What's wrong now?

The HERPETOLOGIST

       (*grunting*)

   I'm stuck in a spider web! You know, there's a species of spider in Australia that can kill a grown man with one bite.

The WOMAN

>But we're not in Australia, are we?

The HERPETOLOGIST

>*(dismissively)*
>
>Tiny detail... tiny detail. Say, can you help me down? I'm afraid of heights.

The WOMAN

>Of course, you are.
>
>>*The WOMAN helps the HERPETOLOGIST down; his snake stick & her cane fall to the ground again.*

The HERPETOLOGIST

>Say, if you're done here... maybe... would you like to share a sandwich?

The WOMAN

>*(dismissively)*
>
>Oh, I don't eat sandwiches.

The HERPETOLOGIST

>What'd'ya have against sandwiches?

The WOMAN

>   Nothing... Maybe I should have said 'I don't eat with strangers'.

The HERPETOLOGIST

>   We wouldn't be strangers if we had lunch together.

The WOMAN

>   Well, we're not having lunch together, so let's just stay strangers.

>   *The HERPETOLOGIST shrugs and surrenders a bit reluctantly.*

The HERPETOLOGIST

>   Well, okay, then. It's been nice chatting with you.

The WOMAN

>   You, too.

The HERPETOLOGIST

>   I'd better get going before that monstrous snake rattles again.

The WOMAN

>   Don't you want to take some measurements or something—I don't know—count her rattles?

The HERPETOLOGIST

> Maybe another time. My nerves are completely shot already. Good luck with your photos.

The WOMAN

> Good luck with your STDs.

The HERPETOLOGIST places the snake stick in her hand and moves to leave when he realizes he's given her the wrong stick. He turns back to swap sticks, but merely studies her silently instead. The WOMAN starts to put her equipment away. Shaking her head, she mumbles to herself.

The WOMAN

> Note to self: make a photo of what it looks like when you're being an idiot. *Let's stay strangers...* brilliant, Captain Mensa!

The WOMAN folds & shoulders her tripod, but is puzzled by her cane. She feels the hook on the other end.

> Rats! He took my cane! I was afraid that would happen.

The HERPETOLOGIST

> Ah hah! I knew you had to be afraid of something! Now, how about that sandwich?

> *Lights down*

The WOMAN

> Alright, I surrender, but we'd better hurry if we wanna avoid that alligator.

The HERPETOLOGIST

> (*alarmed*)

> Alligator?!

> *The end*

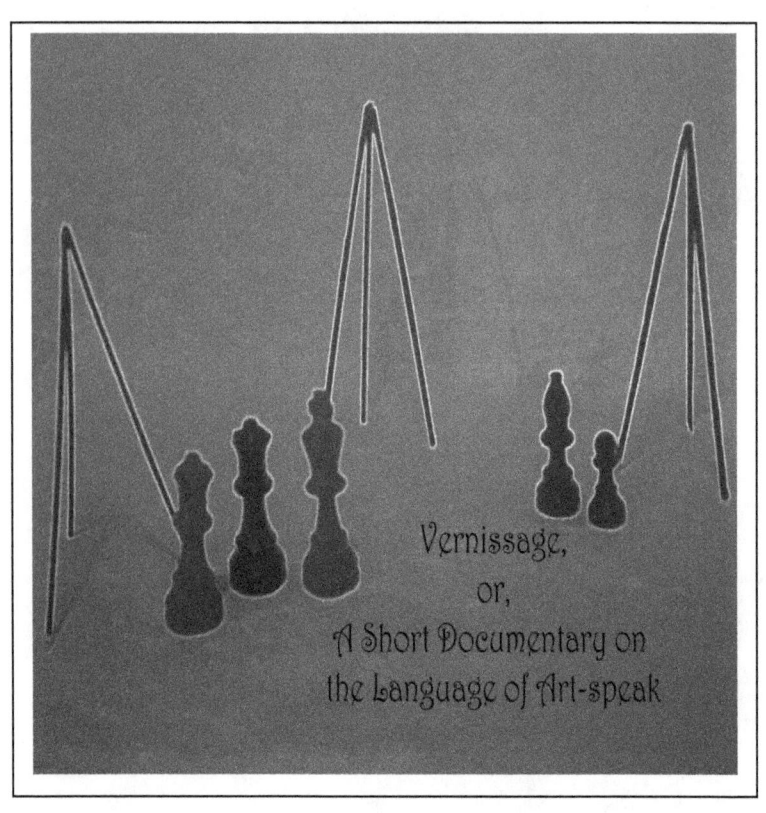

6. Vernissage

Or

A Short Documentary on

The Language of Art-speak

Synopsis: the conversation about the artwork at the Trés Demés gallery reception seems to be about anything but the artwork.

The Cast:

The ARTIST: an up-and-coming artist, comfortably attired in a simple dress & sensible shoes.

KELLY (INGRID): the gallery owner, attired in a sharp skirt & jacket, with an expensive 'do.

HARRISON: a fabulous, hipster gay man & Friend of Kelly (Ingrid)'s, with rainbow hair & a pinstripe suit. He carries a leather shoulder bag with props for the Artist.

NATASCHA: a very young eastern European mail-order bride in a tight black cocktail dress.

BOB: Natascha's older, U.S. husband, down-dressed for casual-Friday, with a surfeit of money but more simple tastes.

The Stage: The Trés Demés art gallery on opening night.

ACT 1

Scene I

Two giant easels stand under spotlights up stage; one more giant easel stands under a spotlight downstage. A single character— the ARTIST— stands in the dark downstage center with her back to the audience. When the lights come up she suddenly turns to face the audience.

The ARTIST

I'm not really like that— what they said about me in the papers. I don't actually speak like that in real life. I'm just a person who likes to make things. I guess I just got some bad advice.

The ARTIST turns her back to the audience again. KELLY (INGRID) enters stage left;

> *the ARTIST turns to meet her. They talk as they walk together toward one of the upstage easels.*

KELLY (INGRID)

> Nobody ever just buys a painting. Our customers— the serious ones, at least— are buying a story & a relationship. The real collectors want to be able to tell their friends they met the artist.

The ARTIST

> They're not gonna name-drop *me*. I'm not anybody...

KELLY (INGRID)

> ... Yet. You're not anybody *yet*, but we're gonna change that, honey, aren't we?

The ARTIST

> I don't know... I mean, y'know, I put a lot of thought into my work. I kinda just wanna let the work speak for itself.

KELLY (INGRID)

> Aw, isn't that sweet. Honey, nobody cares about the thought you put into your work.

The ARTIST

> Yeah, but... these paintings are like my children...

KELLY (INGRID)

> Honey, you wanna be a mommy, or you wanna be successful?

The ARTIST

> Can't I be both?

KELLY (INGRID)

> Not in this business. Trust me: collectors aren't buying art, they're buying the idea of art.

The ARTIST

> What does that even mean?

KELLY (INGRID)

>> (*sighing, taking the ARTIST by both hands, patronizingly*)
>
> Your job, as the *artiste*, is to be awesome. My job, as your agent, is to make you awesome. If you're awesome enough, the customer will write me a really big check, and I'll give you half of it so you

>> (MORE)

KELLY (INGRID) (cont'd)

> can be awesome some more. I hate to burst your bubble, but this is a business...

The ARTIST

> What about my paintings?

KELLY (INGRID)

> The paintings are what we let the customers leave with so they'll feel like they've had an awesome experience.

The ARTIST

>> (*a little disappointed*)
>
> I want people to think my paintings are beautiful...

KELLY (INGRID)

> No, no, no, no, no... You don't ever tell them that. It's like telling them you're an art teacher...

The ARTIST

> ... but I *am* an art teacher.

KELLY (INGRID)

> Honey, *I* know you're an art
>> (MORE)

KELLY (INGRID) (cont'd)

    teacher, and I'm sure you're a wonderful art teacher, but you *never, ever, ever* tell them that... *ever*...

The ARTIST

    Alright, so what am I *s'posed* to say?

KELLY (INGRID)

    Can you do an accent? No, never mind. Just tell them a story about the painting, but be a little opaque. Use words that don't really mean anything: "when my energy is moving through my chakras, I really feel myself entering the canvas," or, "It's so important for our sexually repressive society to see the colours of my pain," that sort of thing.

> *The ARTIST shakes her head in confusion. They both turn away from the audience; KELLY (INGRID) turns back around to face the audience alone.*

(MORE)

KELLY (INGRID) (cont'd)

I've been in the art business forever. My father was Suzie McQueen— yes, *that* Suzie McQueen— so I just about grew up in a gallery. I've seen some good artists... I've seen some great artists. The good ones always make the same mistake: too folksy, too plain, too humble, too "aw, shucks". My job is to help them become truly awesome. Who do you wanna buy art from: your mother sister's cousin, Mabel, or a rock star? This girl may have gotten some bad press, but, by god, she got press! Now, she's like my own personal 401K...

KELLY (INGRID) turns her back to the audience again. As she and the ARTIST turn back around to examine the down stage easel, HARRISON strolls in.

HARRISON

Ingrid! Daaahhhhling!

KELLY (INGRID)

Oh, Harrison, thank god you're
(MORE)

KELLY (INGRID) (cont'd)

here...

> *KELLY (INGRID) & HARRISON exchange air kisses.*

... We're gonna need some backup.

> (*making introductions, to HARRISON*)

Honey, this is my newest talent— we're calling her *Angina*.

> (*to the ARTIST*)

This is one of my oldest friends, Harrison.

The ARTIST

Pleased to meet you.

> *HARRISON takes the ARTIST's hands, turns her left and right, eying her conspicuously.*

HARRISON

Pleasure's all mine, daahhling.

> (*to KELLY (INGRID)*)

Oooh, she's scrumptious! And I just *love* the name. Rhymes with...

The ARTIST

    ... Regina.

HARRISON

    Ewww... boring!

> (*lets go of the ARTIST's hand and promptly ignores her; to KELLY (INGRID)*)

    So, let's get a look at the new work.

KELLY (INGRID)

    The work's *amazing*! It speaks for itself. But Angina's a little...

HARRISON

    ... Rough around the edges?

KELLY (INGRID)

    New. If you can coach her a little on how to sound like an artist...

The ARTIST

    Why can't I just sound like myself?

KELLY (INGRID) & HARRISON

> (*simultaneously*)

    Ugh.

The ARTIST, KELLY (INGRID), & HARRISON turn away from the audience. After a moment, HARRISON turns back to face the audience.

HARRISON

She was, like, straight off the farm, which is totally cute if you're, like, a school teacher or a cleaning lady or something, but she didn't have a clue about the...

(*emphasizes with fingers-quotes*)

... "art world". Maybe once upon a time you could sell art just because it was pretty, but today?! You're competing with the Kardashians, television, movies, the Kardashians, sports, the Kardashians, hip-hop, rap-music, the president, the Kardashians... It's not enough to be good, you gotta be *fah-byu-lous*! I just tried to gay her up a little bit— you know, *Queer Eye for the Boring Painter*!

(*shrugs*)

(MORE)

HARRISON (cont'd)

>She just wasn't ready for the spot-light.

>>*HARRISON turns away from the audience. He, KELLY (INGRID), & the ARTIST turn back & resume their previous activity. HARRISON & the ARTIST move toward the easel upstage left. KELLY (INGRID) strolls to the easel upstage right.*

HARRISON

>Okay, honey, tell me about these paintings. I'll tell you what you're doing wrong.

>>*Enter NATASCHA & BOB, stage right. KELLY (INGRID) intercepts them, approaching NATASCHA.*

KELLY (INGRID)

>>(*in an affected accent*)

>Good evening. Welcome to Trés Demés.

NATASCHA

> (*with a heavy accent*)

Hello, who is owner?

KELLY (INGRID)

I am. My name is Ingrid.

NATASCHA

Oh, okay, vobshche!

BOB

I'm Bob, this is my wife, Natascha. She's not from around here.

KELLY (INGRID)

> (*shaking hands*)

Bienvenu, Bob & Natascha. We're very pleased to be showing the work of avant-gardist Angina, but before we view the collection, can I interest you in some champagne & hors d'oeuvres?

NATASCHA

What kind of champagne is?

KELLY (INGRID)

> Tonight, I'm serving a delicious little Perrier-Jouët Belle Époque...

NATASCHA

> Is Cristal?

KELLY (INGRID)

> No, so sorry, but I'm sure you'll just love the Perrier-Jouët.

NATASCHA

>> (*pouting, whining to BOB*)
>
> Mnye nuzhna Cristal. *Mnye nuzhna!*

BOB

> It's okay, baby: she just didn't understand you. Perrier-Jouët *is* Cristal. Isn't it, Ingrid?

KELLY (INGRID)

> Oops, so sorry, that's what I meant: Perrier-Jouët Cristal... And for you, Bob?

BOB

> Got any beer?

KELLY (INGRID)

>   (*shaking her head*)

Just the Perrier-Jouët Cristal...

>   *On the other side of the stage, HARRISON pulls a purple boa from his bag.*

HARRISON

Let's see if we can dress this up a little bit.

>   *He wraps the boa around the ARTIST's neck & brushes on a raccoon stripe of eye shadow across both eyes & the bridge of her nose. Gazing at her shoes, he shakes his head.*

HARRISON

Let's lose the shoes. Better no shoes than those shoes.

>   *The ARTIST kicks off her shoes, picks them up, & hands them to HARRISON, who eyes them suspiciously & grimaces.*

Oh, honey...

>   *HARRISON fusses with the ARTIST's hair until it*

>   (MORE)

HARRISON (cont'd)

> *resembles a bird's nest.*

There. Oh, you *savage!* Fah-byu-lous!

> *HARRISON notices the clients with KELLY (INGRID).*

We've got a couple of live ones. The girl is status-obsessed, so she's gonna wanna schmooze you, but the guy's got the money, so you need to make your pitch to him. Keep it feminazi-angry, but, y'know, not too angry—just, y'know, opaque, mysterious, whimsical.

The ARTIST

> (*perplexed*)

Whimsical-angry?

HARRISON

> *Stands back, eyes the ARTIST up and down.*

Voila! Oh, Harrison, you're a genius!

> (*to the ARTIST*)

Alright, dahling, it's *showtime!*

>   *KELLY (INGRID) leads NATASCHA*
>   *& BOB over to join HARRISON &*
>   *the ARTIST at an easel.*

KELLY (INGRID)

> *(making introductions)*

Natascha, Bob, this is our artist, Angina.

NATASCHA

> You are painter? Is very nice. I, too, am artist: I am designer.

The ARTIST

> *(genuinely interested)*

Really? What do you design.

NATASCHA

> Mostly outfits... sometimes interior.

The ARTIST

> Where did you go to school?

NATASCHA

> Oh, I not go to school. I learn in gazettye—*Cosmopolitan, Better Home & Garden, HQ*... I love your costume & makeup... vobshche...

HARRISON

>(*flirtatiously*)

Thank you.

> *They all turn away from the audience; NATASCHA turns back & addresses the audience.*

NATASCHA

I like very much these artists. I myself am designer, but in St. Peterburg is still brutalist art. To me is— how you say, happiness?— to meet people who are so amazing— klassna! I think I can be great artist, except in don't know how to make painting or sculpture. What I need is artist who can paint what I tell them. I think maybe this raccoon-girl with feather necklace will do this.

> *NATASCHA turns away from the audience. The entire group turn back to the audience & resume their previous activities. HARRISON sidles up to BOB, looking him up and down.*

HARRISON

> (*flirty*)

Hey, handsome. Casual Friday— such a bold statement.

BOB

Statement?

HARRISON

It says, I have so much money, I don't care what people think.

BOB

I've got no one to impress. Are you Angina's boyfriend?

HARRISON

> (*shocked*)

What?! No!

BOB

Oh, I'm sorry, I didn't mean... I just... you know how things are these days: anyone can be with anybody.

HARRISON

Eeewww!

> (*wanders off in a huff*)

KELLY (INGRID)

> (*leading BOB, NATASCHA, & the ARTIST to the downstage easel*)

Maybe you'd prefer something in more blues & green. Angina, would you like to tell us about this work?

The ARTIST

This one is called *The Shallows*. I was on vacation in Mo'orea...

> *KELLY (INGRID) shakes her head disapprovingly.*

...but who cares about Mo'orea. I...

> (*pauses, sighs, continues blandly*)

... I was escaping the male hegemony, immersing myself in the colours of water where the water signs can truly be free of the prison of our fiery sexuality...

NATASCHA

You are water sign? Me, too! We should paint together someday. I will—how do you say—commission you to make painting with me...

The ARTIST

> (*ignoring NATASCHA, continuing*)

I just let my heart chakra, which is blue...

KELLY (INGRID)

... Throat chakra...

The ARTIST

... throat chakra flow through my veins onto the canvas, which is really just another word for *universe* anyhow...

> *KELLY (INGRID) nods with approval.*

NATASCHA

Tell me about *shallows*.

The ARTIST

Oh, right: it's just about how shallow our culture is in devaluing the individual, especially if you have ovaries, and how we are all only free when we enter the void, where the zodiac defines the blueness of our immersion in...

> (MORE)

The ARTIST (cont'd)
>   (*shaking her head, to KELLY (INGRID)*)

... I forgot where I was going with this, Kelly.

KELLY (INGRID)
>   (*hastily*)

... Ingrid.

The ARTIST

... Ingrid...

NATASCHA

Who is Kelly?

KELLY (INGRID)

No one... So, what do you think about *The Shallows, Natascha*?

NATASCHA
>   (*to the ARTIST*)

I feel Angina & I, we are sisters.

>   (*to KELLY (INGRID)*)

Ingrid, I can really feel this on canvas. This painting I love. I want.

>   (MORE)

NATASCHA (cont'd)
> (*to BOB*)

Honey, I want. You will buy for me?

BOB

Don't you think we should look at the rest of the collection, princess?

NATASCHA
> (*pouting*)

I not want look at rest of collection. I want this water-sign painting with sexual prison...

> *Everyone turns away from the audience. BOB turns back & addresses the audience.*

BOB

I really just wanted a pretty painting for the living room... something beautiful that looked like a place I visited once. What ever happened to landscapes— just nice, simple landscapes? Now everything is *water-signs* & *sexual prisons*. I'm too old for all this... I don't know what I was
> (MORE)

BOB (cont'd)

    thinking, marrying a girl thirty years younger than me— it's exhausting just trying to keep up with her. I can't afford the divorce, so I guess I'll just buy her another painting.

    BOB turns away from the audience; everyone turns back & resumes their previous activity.

KELLY (INGRID)

    What do you think, Bob?

BOB

    How much?

KELLY (INGRID)

    Oh, Bob...

BOB

    How much?

KELLY (INGRID)

    Ten thousand... dollars.

BOB

        (*sighing*)

    Wrap it up.

>   *NATASCHA jumps up and down,
>   pulling on the ARTIST's hand.*

NATASCHA

> Spasibo, spasibo, spasibo! I *love* painting! Next, we work on *my* painting!

KELLY (INGRID)

> Well, let's go pay for this little painting, shall we?

>   *NATASCHA & KELLY (INGRID)
>   exit stage right. BOB & the
>   ARTIST stand uncomfortably in
>   front of the easel a moment
>   or two.*

BOB

>   (*awkwardly*)

> The painting really is very beautiful.

The ARTIST

>   (*very demure &
>   unaffected*)

> Aw, thank you!

BOB

> So, where on Mo'orea were you?

The ARTIST

>We were staying on Ōpūnohu Bay, but on the eastern coast...

BOB

>Where the ferry comes in?

The ARTIST

>North of there, but, yeah. The water was just so beautiful.
>
>*Lights down.*

7. The Nightly News

Synopsis: It's just another day on the nightly news as overpaid, semi-professional anchor Brick Brockman, with the help of his longtime producer & enabler, Carl, lead his savvy co-anchor, Tiffany Andry, Tiffany the weather girl, & Stan Sandy, the sports commentator, through a nightly news broadcast and the personal frictions that transpire during commercial breaks.

The Cast:

BRICK BROCKMAN: the anchor, an older middle aged guy with a bit of narcissism in his closet.

TIFFANY ANDRY: the undervalued co-anchor, a young, lippy journalist who's too smart for the show.

TIFFANY-ON-THE-WEATHER: a young, cute hippy weather-girl who's not a deep thinker & gets by on flirting.

STAN SANDY: on sports, a bored caffeine junky who thinks the news exists for sports.

CARL: the producer, a veteran newsman who's been in the business a little too long, & handles the cue cards for Brick.

*if you have a good performer who just has a little difficulty getting off-book, this play can be set up to cue your actors.

The Stage: The set of a nightly news television show.

ACT I

Scene 1

CARL (OS)

And we're live in three—two—one...

A heroic theme plays briefly. The lights come up on a big desk middle stage center behind which sits BRICK BROCKMAN, the nightly news anchor, with a ridiculous pompadour and an excessively wide tie, staring off in a thoughtful pose stage left. To his left is the smaller desk of TIFFANY ANDRY; to her left the desk of STAN SANDY. To Brockman's right is a tall green-screen in front of which stands TIFFANY-ON-THE-WEATHER. Downstage left is CARL, the cue card guy. BRICK BROCKMAN turns to face the audience with a stern expression.

BRICK BROCKMAM

> Good evening, ladies & gentlemen, & welcome... to *Your News Tonight* with Brick Brockman. I'm your host, Brick Brockman.
>
> > *BRICK BROCKMAN lifts a sheaf of papers from his desk; CARL lifts his oversize cue-boards.*
>
> Our lead story tonight: veteran twenty-something celebrity Mimi Prision went to the playground, but she was not alone. Let's go to Tiffany Andry for the details.
>
> > (*to TIFFANY ANDRY*)
>
> Tiffany?

TIFFANY ANDRY

> That's right Brick. The famed celebrity celebrity, & wife of celebrity *angry rapper* Kandy Kwest, Miss Prision tweeted this morning her intention to take her infant children to a neighborhood playground near their Hightown celebrity mansion. The "private" tweet offered enough forewarning for a mob of celebrity paparazzi to attend the event. With cameras flashing, Miss Prision posted a new selfie to Facespace,

>complaining about all the attention. "Ugh", the post read, "you just can't go anywhere without the whole wolf pack following— sad".
>
>In related news, Miss Prision's sisters, Mindy & Misty, were spotted on Miami Beach riding bicycles in a manner some observers described as "salacious". The younger Prisions are reportedly in the party city working on their tans & more gratuitous attention.
>
>Kandy Kwest could not be reached for comment, but a spokesperson reported that he was angry and would be boycotting the upcoming *Extremely Insulting Lyrics Awards* next week in New York, where he is expected to take top prizes in profanity. Brick.

BRICK BROCKMAN

>Thank you, Tiffany. Tough times for Mimi Prision, eh, Stan?

STAN SANDY

>>(bored, reading paper)
>
>You know what they say, Brick: don't get out of the skillet if

>>(MORE)

STAN SANDY (cont'd)

    you can't stand the fire.

        (*suddenly more animated*)

    Speaking of fire, how about those Angels?

TIFFANY-ON-THE-WEATHER

    Ooh! I *love* angels. I could be your angel, Brick... hehehehe.

        BRICK BROCKMAN *gives TIFFANY-ON-THE-WEATHER a tiny finger-wave;* she blows him a kiss. TIFFANY ANDRY scowls & shakes her head.

BRICK BROCKMAN

    Closer to home, a South City middle school—

        (*squinting at the cue cards*)

    The... Ethel Mermaid Music Magma School...

TIFFANY ANDRY

    I think that's *the Ethel Merman Music Magnate School*, Brick...

BRICK BROCKMAN

    Whatever... was the center of

        (MORE)

BRICK BROCKMAN (cont'd)

    attention today when a grizzly bear made a brief appearance during lunch. Said school principal Edwinna Harper, "We had some moments of sheer terror: I forgot the code to the gun safe, and when I finally got it open, I couldn't find the bullets, but our janitor saved the day." 37 years old Syrian immigrant Omar bin Muham... Muham... Mu...

TIFFANY ANDRY

    Omar bin Muhamad al Farfalla...

BRICK BROCKMAN

    Whatever... lured the dangerous mammal out of the school with a tray of chocolate cupcakes...

TIFFANY-ON-THE-WEATHER

    I *love* chocolate cupcakes...

BRICK BROCKMAN

    We'll have more information as this exciting story unfolds.

        (*BRICK BROCKMAN shuffles some of his papers*)

    In the nation's capitol today, a new kind of gridlock. Here's Tiffany Andry with the details.

TIFFANY ANDRY

That's right, Brick: all traffic ground to a halt on Pennsylvania Avenue after a duck was discovered trying to cross the street with her brood. As motorists left their cars to shoot cute videos of the plucky little hen, D.C. police & National Park Service rangers got into a brawl over whose jurisdiction the offending fowl was in. The traffic snarl lasted several hours, until the Secret Service were able to restore order.

When questioned about the incident, the Speaker of the House said, "It's good to see we're not the only ones causing gridlock here." The Senate Majority Leader protested the remark a few minutes later, tweeting, "It's just inappropriate to try to blame a duck for congressional failures. The speaker's a dope! Sad..." The president has issued a call for hearings into the matter. Meanwhile the spokesperson for celebrity angry rapper Kandy Kwest has refused to comment.

BRICK BROCKMAM

>   Very interesting. Did you know, Tiffany, that ducks mate for life?

TIFFANY ANDRY

>   No, they don't, Brick.

BRICK BROCKAMN

>   Whatever... we'll be back with Tiffany-on-the-Weather after this break.

CARL

>   And we're out. Back in seventy-five, people...

TIFFANY ANDRY

>   (to BRICK BROCKMAN)

>   I can't believe you get paid four times more than me. *Swans* mate for life, you idiot. *Ducks* get roasted with a nice orange glaze.

TIFFANY-ON-THE-WEATHER

>   I'd mate for life, Brick. Hehehe

>   *BRICK BROCKMAN does another little finger-wave.*

TIFFANY ANDRY

>   (shaking her head)

>   Carl...

CARL

    Let's not get sued, Brick.

STAN SANDY

          (*leaning closer to TIFFANY ANDRY*)

    Hey, baby.

TIFFANY ANDRY

    Not if I were threatened with death, Stan.

STAN SANDY

    You and me, baby: the next generation.

TIFFANY ANDRY

          (*snapping*)

    Carl!

CARL

          (*barking*)

    Lawsuit, Stan, lawsuit!

STAN SANDY

          (to BRICK BROCKMAN, who's fluffing his hair)

    Slow news day, Brick?

BRICK BROCKMAN

    Oh, god, what I wouldn't give for a good hurricane or plane crash...

TIFFANY ANDRY

    Nice, Brick: because that wouldn't affect anyone but you, would it?

BRICK BROCKMAN

    I'm just sayin'...

TIFFANY-ON-THE-WEATHER

    I'd love to be in a plane crash with you, Brick. Hehehe.

TIFFANY ANDRY

    I'm sure the rest of us would love that, too, Tiffany...

CARL

    And we're back in three-two-one...

TIFFANY-ON-THE-WEATHER

    Stuff it, Tiffany!

BRICK BROCKMAN

        (*flustered*)

    Uh... uh... well, it's a beautiful day to go to the beach and work on your tan, and here with the weather, our own beautiful, tanned Tiffany-on-the-Weather...

TIFFANY-ON-THE-WEATHER

> (*cooing at BRICK BROCKMAN*)

Thanks, Brick, and may I just say, that tie looks so *sexy* on you, you hunka-hunka burnin' love!

> BRICK BROCKMAN does another finger wave; TIFFANY-ON-THE-WEATHER turns her attention to the green screen and gestures flirtatiously.

So, the word of the day is *hot... hot... hot...*

BRICK BROCKMAN

I'll say!

STAN SANDY

Uh huh, oh, yeah!

TIFFANY-ON-THE-WEATHER

With a high-pressure system sitting right over top of us, and clear skies, the temp is going up... up... up. Not to worry: when this line of clouds sweeps in, we can expect some clouds, maybe a little precip in the form of rain, and a nice breeze to cool things off.

(MORE)

TIFFANY-ON-THE-WEATHER (cont'd)

> *She suggestively bends at the waste, purses her lips, and blows across the green screen.*

Hehehehe

BRICK BROCKMAN

> (*shifts in his seat uncomfortably*)

Oh, my.

STAN SANDY

> (*leaning forward*)

That's what I'm talking about.

TIFFANY ANDRY

> (*scowling*)

And what's the u.v. index, Tiffany?

TIFFANY-ON-THE-WEATHER

> (annoyed, but unctuously, *at TIFFANY ANDRY*)

It's hot, and there's no shade. What'd'you think, *Tiffany*?

> (MORE)

TIFFANY-ON THE-WEATHER (cont'd)

>   (*to the audience again*)

To deal with any heat-related health effect from the heat, the city has announced that they will be keeping recreation & senior centers open for extended hours through the week, and the Red Cross will be giving away free water, so if you're feeling the signs of heat protesta... protestate... pros... prostate...

TIFFANY ANDRY

That's prostration, I'm pretty sure, Tiffany...

BRICK BROCKMAN

Whatever...

TIFFANY-ON-THE-WEATHER

...Prostration, be sure to check in for relief. Back to you, Brick.

>   (*winks at BRICK BROCKMAN*)

BRICK BROCKMAN

>   (*cooing*)

Well, that's excellent, Tiffany, just excellent.

TIFFANY-ON-THE-WEATHER

>Thanks, Brick. Maybe we could get together later for a personal critique of my work.

BRICK BROCKMAN

>And speaking of relief, let's head over to Stan Sandy at our sports desk and hear about the Angels' new "relief" pitcher.

TIFFANY-ON-THE-WEATHER

>Oh, I *love* angels...

STAN SANDY

>>(*suddenly animated*)

>Thanks, Brick. Well, the Angels don't have a new relief pitcher, but baseball's been in the news this week in a big way as the city has announced a brand new, publicly funded stadium for our beloved team. The three trillion-dollar project, funded on a ten percent increase in sales tax throughout the state, promises better V.I.P. seating, a helipad for V.I.P. arrivals & departures, &, perhaps best of all, a state-of-the-art media suite for sports casters.

BRICK BROCKMAN

    And what do the team owners think of these improvements, Stan?

STAN SANDY

    Thanks for asking that, Brick. There was some concern by management that they would be asked to buy in, but generous gifts to the city council have minimized corporate investment in the project. The team's owner, 67-year-old Vincent Fussel, on vacation in Monaco with his new wife, the 19-year-old super model Tiffany Tahler, was unavailable for comment. A spokesperson for the corporate office issued this statement:

    "Given the enormous amount of prestige that comes to the city from our team's presence here, we feel this is an appropriate investment in the future of the team and this city."

BRICK BROCKMAN

    Media suite? Sweet! Will you be inviting colleagues to join you, Stan?

STAN SANDY

>   (*ogling TIFFANY ANDRY*)

>   I sure hope so, Brick.

BRICK BROCKMAN

>   It's time for another brief message from our sponsors. When we're back, Tiffany Andry has the scoop on a new high school music program. Stay with us!

CARL

>   And we're out. Sixty seconds, people...

TIFFANY-ON-THE-WEATHER

>   What's an s.u.v. index?

BRICK BROCKMAN & STAN SANDY

>   (*at once*)

>   Ah, it's nothin'. Don't worry about it, honey.

CARL

>   Attention, people. The news director wants somebody to cover the Euthanasia convention tomorrow.

TIFFANY-ON-THE-WEATHER

>   Do we get to *go* to Asia?

CARL

> (*ignoring TIFFANY-ON-THE-WEATHER, looks at TIFFANY ANDRY*)

Tif?

BRICK BROCKMAN

> Aw, c'mon Carl. How come she gets all the cherries?

TIFFANY ANDRY

> Because he needs someone who can *spell* cherries, Brick.

BRICK BROCKMAN

> Whatever... let me go instead.

CARL

> Thanks, Tif. I'll set you up with Andy for camera & Frank for production.

TIFFANY ANDRY

> I don't suppose we have any female cameramen or producers?

TIFFANY-ON-THE-WEATHER

> Uh, *duh!* If we had any *female* cameramen, they'd be called camera*women*, wouldn't they, *Tif?*

TIFFANY ANDRY

> (*surprised*)
> Huh... you're right.

CARL

> And we're back in three—two—one...

TIFFANY-ON-THE-WEATHER

> Stuff it, Tiffany!

BRICK BROCKMAN

> When violin virtuoso Yitzak Korngold emigrated to the U.S. seventy years ago, he never dreamed how successful he'd become. Now, the 85-year-old musician wants to give back to his community with a unique new music program in our public schools. Here's Tiffany Andry with the details.

TIFFANY ANDRY

> Thanks, Brick. That's right: when the celebrated octogenarian German émigré recently attended the holiday concert at the school of his great grand daughter, Tiffany Korngold, he was shocked to discover a near total absence of music in the program. "It was all sarcasm," Korngold told us over the phone, "like shockingly rude

vaudeville put on by poorly dressed little kids. I thought, 'I did not survive the holocaust to see this happen'". Now, the award-winning musician is rallying the arts & entertainment community to get involved. "A world without music is a world without a soul," said Korngold "The violin has save my life. Before I die, I just want to put violins back in school." Celebrity angry rapper Kandy Kwest could not be reached for comment.

BRICK BROCKMAN

Very heartwarming, Tiffany.

TIFFANY-ON-THE-WEATHER

I don't know, Brick. I think it's terrible. Don't we already have enough violence in the schools?

TIFFANY ANDRY

Violins, Tiffany! Violins!

> BRICK BROCKMAN smiles at TIFFANY-ON-THE-WEATHER, shakes his head adorably, & finger-waves; she blows him a kiss.

TIFFANY ANDRY

Brick?

BRICK BROCKMAN

> (*distracted*)
>
> Yeah? Oh...
>
> (*turns back to the audience*)
>
> Uh... so what do you do when you already have everything? The adventure travel company *Ennui* is trying to answer this question. Here's our very own Miss Andry...

TIFFANY ANDRY

> (*annoyed*)
>
> ... *again*...

BRICK BROCKMAN

> ... With the story.

TIFFANY ANDRY

> What do you get the person who has everything? How about a trip to nowhere? That's right, adventure travel pioneers *Ennui*, who have brought us such tours as *That's MY Volcano* Bikram spelunking & *Freezin' My You-know-what Off* Arctic kayaking, is introducing their new line, *Peoria, Where?*, promising two weeks of overpriced, excruciating boredom. Company executives say the new trend...

BRICK BROCKMAN

>(*interrupting*)

Oops, I'm sorry, Tiffany, but it's time for another message from our sponsors. Stay tuned for more of *Your Nightly News*, with me, Brock Brickman...

TIFFANY ANDRY

>(*exasperated*)

That's *Brick Brockman, Brick*...

BRICK BROCKMAN

Whatever...

CARL

And we're out... Ninety seconds, people.

>*Lights out.*

CARL (VO)

Tonight's show brought to you by Preparation H: when you're burning up, and Preparations A through G just aren't enough...

8. On the Bus...

Synopsis: It's a nice day for a ride. As Bud the Driver guides his bus around the city streets, his buddy Teddy drops in on the private conversations of his fellow passengers; but are they as random as they seem?

The Cast:

BUD: a middle-aged, career bus driver.

TEDDY: a bored busybody who makes a living suing people.

OPIE: a big guy with a hard-hat.

CARLY: a young woman from the U.S.

FRANZ: a German émigré with broken English, Carly's "green-card" husband.

RED: Rusty "RED" Knape, a loud, conservative guy with a pronounced country accent.

SANDY: RED's companion, also conservative & country.

The Stage: a public transportation bus.

ACT I

Scene 1

BUD (OS)

    Next stop, 15&53rd.

        Lights up.

        Downstage center, from stage right, lined up in pairs facing stage left, eight chairs, in one of the two rearmost of which sits TEDDY, casually dressed, with a notebook in his lap. One more chair sits slightly forward of the others, slightly upstage, occupied by BUD, the driver, in his uniform & cap, &, in front of BUD is a huge, loose steering wheel.

TEDDY

    There's nobody on the bus, Bud. Exactly who are you making announcements for?

BUD

    Well, *you're* on the bus, Teddy...

TEDDY

    How long I been ridin' your bus you don't know I don't get off here?

BUD

    I know you don't get off here, but sometimes I have passengers who do.

TEDDY

    So why not save it for them?

BUD

    It's a habit, Teddy, like using the blinkers.

TEDDY

    I swear, Bud: you must be the last person left in the country who uses blinkers.

BUD

    That's not true: there's a person right in front of me with his blinker on.

TEDDY

> (looking at his empty book)

Well, that's two o' ya.

BUD

> (to himself)

Somebody's cranky today.

> (to TEDDY)

Did we forget our coffee?

> *The bus stops. BUD opens the door and waits while OPIE, a big fellow in a hard-hat & dirty clothes boards carrying a bag of food.*

BUD

Opie.

OPIE

Bud. Hey, Teddy.

> *OPIE takes a seat right behind BUD, who closes the door and steers.*

BUD

Teddy's in a mood today. He's not sayin' much.

OPIE

>What's the matter, Teddy? Forget your coffee? Say, Bud, you mind if I eat my lunch?

BUD

>Just don't leave any crumbs. I hate it when you guys make a mess in my bus. Next stop, 23& 53rd...

>>*OPIE removes a sub sandwich and a soda from the bag and starts eating.*

TEDDY

>No one's gettin' off there, either, Bud.

BUD

>>(*to OPIE*)

>See?

TEDDY

>>(*fanning the air with his book*)

>Man, Ope! You have to eat that thing in here? Now the whole bus smells like a Subway.

OPIE

>>(*biting off a hunk of*
>>(MORE)

OPIE (cont'd)
> *sandwich, talking with his mouth full*)

Mmmm, delicious! Want some, Ted?

TEDDY

Disgusting.

OPIE

What're we writin' today?

TEDDY

Nothin' yet. Everybody's been boring.

OPIE

You want I should tell ya a story, Teddy?

TEDDY

I want you should not exhale while you're eatin' *that* disgusting mess.

BUD

There once was a writer named Teddy, who kept his pen at the ready, but Opie ate cheese, causing Teddy to sneeze, and he missed a good story instead-y.

OPIE

    Good one, Bud. Write that, Ted.

TEDDY

    That's stupid. *Insteady*? It's not even a word.

BUD

    See? Grumpy.

OPIE

    Geeze.

> *The bus stops; BUD effects to open the door, & waits as a youngish couple—CARLY & FRANZ—get on.*

FRANZ

        (*with a thick accent*)

    Hallo, Mr. Bus-driver. Hallo, Mr. Passenger.

> *FRANZ pays BUD, who closes the door as they pass.*

BUD

    Next stop, 31 & 53rd.

> *Waving at the air in front of them as they walk past OPIE, CARLY & FRANZ take the two seats in front of TEDDY.*

FRANZ

>   Hallo, Mr. Other-passenger.

CARLY

>   (*apologetically*)
>
>   Don't mind him: he's not from around here.

FRANZ

>   (*picking up where he'd left off before boarding the bus*)
>
>   So, this tiny little fat lady—she is like Hitler's mother—she starts pointing at me a pen und yelling, 'Behind the line! Behind the line!' as if she were starting a race...

CARLY

>   It's the HIPAA law…

FRANZ

>   Ja-ja, this is what she is yelling at me, 'The hippo! The hippo!', und I am asking what is this with the hippopotamus in the pharmacy?

CARLY

>   No, "hipaa"—health insurance privacy act act— hipaa something or another, I don't know...

FRANZ

> Ja-ja! Ich verstehen! But this fat little pen-woman, she is yelling me this line is to keep the hippopotamus back. I say to her, but this is pharmacy, not a zoo-park. Why there are all the hippos & rhinos?

CARLY

> (*sighing*)
>
> It's not hip... oh, never mind.

>> *TEDDY is interested and leans over his seat to eaves-drop.*

TEDDY

> So, what happened next?

CARLY

> Don't encourage 'im, *please*.

FRANZ

> (*growing excited*)
>
> What happens next? I will tell you what happens next: she was very insolent! She told me I should learn to speak the English. 'Yes,' I told her, 'I am speaking th'English. What language you are speaking?' I say to her.

TEDDY

>(*scribbling in his notebook, to himself*)

This is great!

>(*to FRANZ & CARLY*)

So, who *are* you guys?

CARLY

Why? You writin' a book?

TEDDY

No, I'm a playwright. My name's Teddy.

FRANZ

What kind of plays you are writing?

TEDDY

I write short plays, but not about boring stuff. I like to write 'slice of life' stuff— y'know, like, totally random people you meet on a bus.

FRANZ

Have we ever seen your plays that you writed?

TEDDY

>   Oh, I don't know. I'm not very famous...

OPIE

>   ... Yet. He's not famous yet. But y' never know.

BUD

>   Teddy writes a new play every week, based on what he sees on my bus.

OPIE

>   Tell 'em about *Two Guys Comparing Scars*... from mosquito bites...

BUD

>   It's just like a scene outa *Jaws*, only better.

TEDDY

>   Nah. I couldn't make that one work.

BUD

>   Yeah, me, neither.

FRANZ

>   So, now you are writing a play about us?

TEDDY

> Maybe. I'm always looking for interesting characters, and you guys are interesting.

OPIE

> Maybe you should just leave 'em alone, Teddy.

FRANZ

> No, no, this is interesting. So, tell me, Mister Play-man, what kind of play you will write about me?

CARLY

> It's a comedy: a German goes to a pharmacy and thinks it's a zoo.

FRANZ

> Well... you don't know what you will find at United States pharmacy. In Germany, you go to the chemist for medicine. In U.S., you buy pills und toilet paper und toys und ket food...

TEDDY

> *Ket* food?

FRANZ

> Ja...

TEDDY

    You said 'ket food'...

FRANZ

    Ja...

CARLY

    He means 'cat food'.

FRANZ

    This is what I say. *Ket food.*

        BUD effects to open the door, letting on RED & SANDY.

BUD

    Next stop, 38 & 53rd.

FRANZ

    Why does the chemist carry ket food? Is this medicine? No...

        BUD closes the door. RED pays, & he & SANDY, who wave the air in front of them as they pass OPIE & his smelly sandwich, take the seats immediately in front of FRANZ & CARLY.

TEDDY

    You can't get cat food in a pharmacy in Germany?

FRANZ

    No! No! In Germany, you go to the druggist for *druks*. You go to the department store for the ket food.

RED

    (*to SANDY, loudly*)

    Sounds like some o' them foreigners got on our bus.

    (*to OPIE*)

    You ain't a foreigner, is ya?

OPIE

    (*through a mouthful of sandwich, shaking his head*)

    Opie, pleased t' meet ya.

RED

    (*to SANDY*)

    See: Amurikin.

    (*to OPIE*)

    I'm Rusty... Rusty Knape... but everyone calls me Red.

OPIE

    Red Knape: got it. What kinda name is that?

RED

    The 'Murikin kind. It's spelled with a "k", but the "k"'s silent, like knock.

SANDY

    His brother prenounces it Kah-Nah-Pay, but he's a fruitcup— he gotta do ev'rythang fancy.

RED

    (*to OPIE, waves the air*)

    Dang, son: that thang's offensive.

OPIE

    (*waving the air*)

    Sorry, I only got ten minutes to eat lunch.

TEDDY

    (*to CARLY & FRANZ*)

    Where're you guys from?

CARLY

    St.Petersburg...

SANDY

    Ruski! See: *foreigners*.

CARLY

    ... Florida.

TEDDY

    Franz?

FRANZ

    I... Well, I was born in Unter-Aden-Baden-Wurtzen-Sturzen-Heim, but when I was teenager we move, my family and I, up the hill to Ober-Aden-Baden-Wurtzen-Sturzen-Heim.

> *TEDDY is trying to keep up with FRANZ in his notebook.*

TEDDY

    Sheesh, that's a mouthful.

FRANZ

    It was longer once. I don't know why it is shortened. What ist this 'fruitcup'?

> *CARLY poses an effeminate gesture. FRANZ is shocked and glances with disapproval at RED & SANDY.*

    Oh! This is not nice!

TEDDY

> Have we met before?

CARLY

> Why? Do we look familiar?

OPIE

> Everybody looks the same to Ted. Don't they, Ted.

TEDDY

> I never forget a face. Remembering faces is my superpower.

CARLY

> Maybe we met on the bus? I mean, an earlier time, or somethin'.

TEDDY

> No, I'd remember that. So, this Ober-Aden-Baden...

FRANZ

> ...Wurtzen-Sturzen-Heim?

TEDDY

> Yeah. It's in Germany?

FRANZ

> It's in Bayern...

CARLY

> ... Bavaria...

FRANZ

> ... which is in southern Germany.

SANDY

> (*loudly*)
>
> See: *foreigner*, just like I said.

RED

> He's prob'ly collectin' the social security.

TEDDY

> (*obviously ignoring RED & SANDY*)
>
> How'd you two meet?

FRANZ

> I made an advertisement in the paper.

TEDDY

> What... like a personal add or something?

FRANZ

> Ja, ja. What is this, 'personal ad'?

CARLY

    Yeah, like a personal.

FRANZ

    I offer ten thousand euros for a wife for U.S. green card— which, by the way, is actually pink.

> *BUD stops the bus, effects to open & close the door, admitting no one new, then drives on.*

BUD

    Next stop: Bell & 72nd.

TEDDY

    So, you're married.

CARLY

    (grabbing FRANZ's arm affectionately)

    We're very happy together.

FRANZ

    Ja, I should say for ten thousand euros. I need a wife for the pink green-card.

CARLY

>I'm not really his type.

TEDDY

>Who is?

FRANZ

>>(*staring hard at RED & SANDY*)
>
>I'm a fruitcup!

RED

>>(*to SANDY, loudly*)
>
>Great! Just what we need in the good ole U.S. of A. is another hoe-moe-sekshel.

FRANZ

>>(*agitated*)
>
>At least this German queer won't be waving around the tik-teks und trumping her greb-thing!

TEDDY

>*Greb-thing*?

CARLY

>He means 'grab-thing'.

FRANZ

    Her *ket*! These people— they eat tik-teks und greb the ket!

CARLY

    He means 'pussy'...

FRANZ

    Ja-ja! Poor pussy-ket!

SANDY

    Who was talkin' t' *you*? Why don't ya mind yer own bidness, *Fritz*.

FRANZ

    Franz!

RED

    Yeah, whatever.

SANDY

    At least my Red know how t' trump a grab-thang!

RED

    ... 'Murikin as apple pah.

OPIE

    So how 'bout those Patriots?

RED & SANDY

> (*instantly losing interest in FRANZ & CARLY*)

Oh, that was one heck of a game!

RED

That Tom Brady is like the all-time best football player of all time!

SANDY

And he's handsome, t' boot!

RED

> (*looking suddenly shocked*)

Never you mind, now, *he's handsome*. He put his pants on one leg at a time just like me.

> (*to OPIE*)

You kin tell a lot 'bout a country by what kinda sports it plays.

SANDY

We don't play no soccer here, no sir!

RED

> We play red-blooded, Amurikin sports— football, an' Nascar, 'n' hockey...

OPIE

> Well... hockey's Canadian, y'know.

RED

> Well, so is Shatner, but if ya close yer eyes you kin pretend like Canady's just the 51st state...

SANDY

> ... 51st *commie* state...

RED

> Like Califor-neye-yay, only with snow.

SANDY

> Shatner. Now, there's a man who knows how t' trump some grab-thang! & Fat Albert...

RED

> Now, not him, honey: he's a African...

FRANZ

>   (*to TEDDY*)

>   Oh, mein gott: how this is going to make America great again, tell me?

TEDDY

>   (*enthusiastically*)

>   Maybe it's not, but I got some *great* material!

>   *TEDDY looks up from his book.*

TEDDY

>   Awe, nuts. This is my stop. Here's my phone number. Why don't you call me— we can have lunch.

FRANZ

>   Und then I will be character in your comedy-play?

TEDDY

>   Yeah! Call me!

>   *BUD effects to open the door and waits while TEDDY collects his things & exits. BUD closes the door & steers the bus back into traffic.*

BUD

    Next stop, 46 & 83rd

        There are a few moments of silence as the bus moves along.

FRANZ

        (*with no accent*)

    That okay, Bud?

BUD & OPIE

        (*talking over each other enthusiastically*)

    That was *great*! You guys were terrific!

        CARLY, FRANZ, RED, & SANDY high-five each other.

RED

    'Trump my grab-thing'! Did you write that, Bud?

BUD

    No, Sandy came up with that one when we were brainstorming the other night.

RED & OPIE

    Good one, girl!

        Sandy bows from her seat.

CARLY

> (*laughing*)

Tik-teks!

BUD

I'll make some notes tonight, but you guys were great, thanks!

RED

Hey, Bud, can I play the German guy next time? I got a good German accent.

BUD

How about *Indian*? I'm working on a play for next week called *Tech Support*. Can ya do an Indian accent?

RED

> (*shaking his tic-tacs, with an Indian accent*)

Hallo, my name is Rajiv. May I please be Trumping your grab-thing, thank you very much?

> *Lights down.*

OPIE

Hey, Bud, how many more times you think we can do this before Teddy catches on?

9. G_O_O_M_B_A_S!

Synopsis: Big J and Rocko wait in a car in a tiny town, on a mission to "whack" some unsuspecting victim. To kill the time, they work on the Sunday crossword puzzle. When the Godmother calls to find out where they are, some confusion ensues.

The Cast:

BIG J: a middle-management mob boss on a job in Gulfport, Florida, who's not as smart as he thinks he is.

ROCKO: the "muscle" for Big J, who doesn't seem too bright, but is aces at the crossword puzzle.

The GODMOTHER: the "big boss", a little old lady in big glasses, sensible shoes, & a mean streak.

The Stage: Two chairs side by side downstage left, where ROCKO sits behind a steering wheel, and BIG J sits on a big pile of bubble wrap. Partition, center stage. A big easy chair, a small table with a rotary phone, & floor lamp upstage right.

ACT I

Scene 1

BIG J sits in the passenger seat on a pile of bubble wrap, writing on a section of folded newspaper; ROCKO sits in the driver seat, with a steering wheel resting on the floor in front of him. ROCKO is reading from a letter.

ROCKO

    (*thick mafia accent*)

Hey, did you know that Charlie won an all-expense-paid cruise? Yeah, he says here, he's goin' to Mexico.

BIG J

    (*thick mafia accent*)

Charlie Shoes? That's great. Why do I care?

    (MORE)

BIG J (cont'd)

> (*to himself*)
>
> Seven-eight-nine… nine letters, starts with a "Q"?

ROCKO

> Uh-oh, apparently the radio station called Charlie about the cruise, but they got Mrs. Charlie instead, and she didn't know anything about it, and he'd already asked that Zelda-girl down at the club.

BIG J

> Same old Charlie Shoes.
>
> (*to himself*)
>
> Day-to-day... nine letters, starts with a "Q".

ROCKO

> He better watch out: Mrs. Charlie's in tight with the Boss. He don't wanna get whacked over no cruise with that Zelda-girl.

BIG J

> Will you knock it off with the jibber jabber already. This is the Sunday New York times crossword puzzle.

ROCKO

> Meaning what?

BIG J

> Meaning it's hard, and I can't concentrate with you going on about Charlie Shoes's cruises and the women who are gonna whack 'im.

ROCKO

> Sorry, boss.
>
> > (*pause*)
>
> Quotidian.

BIG J

> Huh?

ROCKO

> Quotidian, q_u_o_t_i_d_i_a_n, quotidian.

BIG J

> What the heck are you talking about.

ROCKO

> Day-to-day, nine letters, starts with a "Q": quotidian.

BIG J

> > (*scribbling in the*
> > (MORE)

BIG J (cont'd)

> *paper*)
>
> I'll be darned: it fits. How the heck do you know what quotidian means? You never even read a book!

ROCKO

> I read a book.

BIG J

> Oh, yeah? What book you ever read, Rocko?

ROCKO

> I read a book, and I watch the Jeopardy with my ma. You can learn a lot from the Jeopardy: that Alex Trebek, he's a pretty smart guy.
>
> (*pause*)
>
> He's Canadian, you know.

BIG J

> What's that s'posed to mean?

ROCKO

> It's just that, we get a lot of our entertainment from Canadia.

BIG J

> No, we don't: the entertainment, that's all Jews and homosexuals.

ROCKO

        (*after a pause*)

What about Keanu Reeves?

BIG J

Keanu Reeves is a Jew?

ROCKO

No, Keanu Reeves is a Canadian.

BIG J

No, he ain't...

ROCKO

        (*nodding*)

Born & bred.

BIG J

No, that ain't so. That's fake news.

ROCKO

No, it's true— played hockey 'n everything.

BIG J

Hockey, huh?

ROCKO

Keanu Reeves is Canadian, Donald Sutherland, Ann Margaret, even Shattner.

BIG J

    No, not Shattner!

ROCKO

    Yup: Shattner.

BIG J

    Oh, man, not Shattner.

        Glancing out the window, BIG J gets excited.

    Ooh, Rocko: that's the guy... I think that's the guy.

ROCKO

        (*looking at a photo*)

    I don't know, boss: it don't look very much like the guy in the picture.

BIG J

    Lemme see.

ROCKO

        (*showing the photo*)

    See: the guy in the picture is white. That guy's black.

BIG J

        (*squinting*)

    I don't know.

ROCKO

> You want I should whack 'im? We still got room in the trunk.

BIG J

> Nah— you already whacked the wrong guy three times, and one of them guys was a woman.

ROCKO

> Me?! You were the one who told me to whack 'em.
>
> *BIG J struggles to straighten his bubble wrap, studies the newspaper.*

BIG J

> 'Like a tove'. What the heck is a 'tove'?

ROCKO

> (*grumbling*)
>
> I was only followin' orders.
>
> (*pause*)
>
> Six letters?

BIG J

> What?

ROCKO

> Six letters? 'Like a tove'... is it six letters?

BIG J

> Four-five-six... yeah, six letters.

ROCKO

> Slythy... s_l_y_t_h_y... slythy.

> *BIG J writes in the letters.*

BIG J

> What the heck is a *slythy tove*?

ROCKO

> I don't know.

BIG J

> What'd'ya mean, 'you don't know'? How do you know it's a slythy tove if you don't know what a slythy tove is?

ROCKO

> It's from the poem.

BIG J

> Poem? What Poem? You never read no poem!

ROCKO

> I did so read a poem. It's from "Jabberwocky", by Lewis Carroll.

BIG J

> Lewis Carroll. You mean the old guy who played Topper?

ROCKO

> Topper? What? No... the guy who wrote "Alice in Wonderland".

BIG J

> You mean the movie with the smilin' cat?

ROCKO

> Well, you know, that was a book.

BIG J

> (*to himself*)
>
> That must be the one book you read.

ROCKO

> What's that, boss?

BIG J

> Nothin'. Now I'm all curious what a slythy tove is.

ROCKO

> It ain't nothing— it's just nonsense: "'Twas brillig, and the slythy toves did gyre and gimble in the wabe; all mimsy were the borogoves, and the mome raths outgrabe"...

BIG J

> Aw, c'mon. Now you are reciting poetry?

ROCKO

> I'm tellin' ya, boss: it's the Jeopardy. I think you can get smart by the osmosis.

BIG J

> Is that how you learned about all them Canadians?

ROCKO

> Well, no. I also watch Entertainment Tonight with my ma. She likes the celebrity gossip from that Perez Hilton.

BIG J

> Is that the chick with the hotel chain and the pornos?

ROCKO

> No, that's *Paris* Hilton. Perez is the gay.

BIG J

> See, now: this is the kind a jibber-jabber I wanted to avoid. Why don't you look out for our mark, & I'll finish this puzzle.
>
>> (*to himself*)
>
> 'Possible pumice plumes'.

ROCKO

> Six letters?

BIG J

> Shut up!
>
>> (*to himself*)
>
> Five-six...
>
>> (*to ROCKO*)
>
> Alright, what is it?

ROCKO

> Does tephra fit?

BIG J

> Ha! Six letters, wise-guy! Six!

ROCKO

> T_e_p_h_r_a... tephra.

> *BIG J scribbles irritably, then adjusts his bubble wrap.*

BIG J

    Unbelievable.

ROCKO

    Sorry, boss. How are them piles?

BIG J

    We're sittin' in a car for hours and hours. How do you think they are?

ROCKO

    Sorry, boss.

BIG J

    Thank you. Now, shut up and watch the street.

        (*to himself*)

    Thirty-seven acrost: 'gauche over tiny bits?' What the heck is that s'posed to mean?

> *BIG J glances at ROCKO, who shifts awkwardly in his seat.*

    You know, this is a very hard puzzle.

ROCKO

>	Bill Clinton does it in an hour... in pen.

BIG J

>	Yeah, well, I ain't no Bill Clinton. You don't see me getting' my cigar stuck...

ROCKO

>	All I'm sayin' is, he's a smart guy. And you *can't* get your cigar stuck, on account of your asthma.

BIG J

>	Never you mind my asthma. If I *could* smoke a cigar, at least I know which end to light.

ROCKO

>	Oh, I think he does, too, boss. You know, he's a Rhodes Scholar?

BIG J

>	Is that somethin' else you got off the Jeopardy?

ROCKO

>	No, but I bet he'd be good at the Jeopardy. Say, what's the title of the puzzle.

BIG J

> What? I don't know.

ROCKO

> Here, let me see.
>
> *BIG J holds the paper for ROCKO to see.*
>
> 'Questions, Fermi'... ah, got it.

BIG J

> 'Gauche...' man, that's a lot of letters... sixteen.
>
> *ROCKO fidgets in his seat and glances around; BIG J eyes him with growing frustration.*
>
> Fine, Captain Mensa. You think you know the answer? Let 'er rip.

ROCKO

> (*sighing with relief*)
>
> Tacky-on-particles... t_a_c_k_y_o_n_p_a_r_t_i_c_l_e_s... tacky-on-particles.
>
> *BIG J scribbles hastily to keep up.*

BIG J

> There is no way this is right... rats! It fits! Okay, tell me: how the heck did you get *that*?

ROCKO

> So, the name of the puzzle is 'Questions, Fermi', get it? Questions, Fermi... Enrico Fermi...

BIG J

> Is this another Canadian on the Paris Hilton show?

ROCKO

> What? No... no, he's one of us...

BIG J

> Cosa nostra?

ROCKO

> No, Italian. He's a nucular physicist, made the first nucular reactor, and, of course, tachyons are particles... theoretical particles that can move faster that light... so, 'gauche over tiny bits'... get it?

>> *BIG J stares slack-jawed at ROCKO.*

> 'Gauche'—tacky... 'tiny bits'... Fermi, get it?

BIG J

>> (*astonished*)
>> (MORE)

BIG J (cont'd)

And you got all that off the Jeopardy?

(*shaking his head*)

Jeez, Rocko. I don't even know what goes on in that head of yours.

BIG J suddenly grabs his pants, extracting his mobile phone from his pocket. He glances at it, then at ROCKO, vexed.

Uh-oh... it's the boss.

ROCKO

Uh-oh: I hope we don't gotta push the button on Charlie Shoes. I like Charlie Shoes, & I ain't never had to whack nobody I knew before.

BIG J

(*to ROCKO*)

Shut up, already.

(*answering the phone*)

Hi, boss.

The lights come up on the easy chair stage right, where a little old lady— the

GODMOTHER— in giant glasses and sensible shoes holds the receiver of a black rotary phone to her ear.

GODMOTHER

(*heavy mafia accent*)

Hello Big J. How's it goin' down there?

BIG J

Oh, it's... it's... it's goin' great, Godmother, just great.

GODMOTHER

How's your partner? Is he with you?

BIG J

Oh, yes ma'am. He's drivin'.

GODMOTHER

Are yous drivin' right now?

BIG J

No, ma'am. We are conducting surveillance, Godmother. We are hot on the trail of our bird... your bird.

GODMOTHER

Tell me, Big J, have you whacked anyone yet?

BIG J

> Uh, well, in a manner of speaking, ma'am, yes, we have...

GODMOTHER

> How many people have yous two whacked?

BIG J

> Well, uh, guys— total, uh, two...

GODMOTHER

> TWO! And are either of these guys my guy, Big J?

BIG J

> Uh, we think probably not, ma'am: the one appears to be a Mexican, and the other, we think, was a Sikh.

GODMOTHER

> A Sikh, huh.

BIG J

> Yup, turban and everything. We thought he might be in disguise. Same thing with the woman— we thought maybe he was in drag...

GODMOTHER

> WOMAN! You whacked a woman?

BIG J

> We thought she might be a guy... our guy... your guy.

GODMOTHER

> Have you disposed of the stiffs?

BIG J

> Oh, yes, ma'am: we got rid of 'em right away.

GODMOTHER

> Should I ask where you knuckleheads have disposed of your trail of bodies?

BIG J

> They're in the trunk.

GODMOTHER

> OF YOUR CAR!?

BIG J

> Well, we didn't wanna stash 'em in the trunk of somebody else's car, boss.

GODMOTHER

> Is that sarcasm, Big J? I surely hope that is not sarcasm.

BIG J

    Oh, no ma'am.

        (*pause*)

    Ma'am?

GODMOTHER

    Big J, let me ask ya, where are yous right now?

BIG J

    We're parked in front of an Italian restaurant. We figured that was the most likely place to spot our guy... your guy.

GODMOTHER

    Uh-huh. And where is this restaurant located, Big J?

BIG J

    Right on the main street, Godmother.

GODMOTHER

    Uh-huh. And where is this main street located, Big J?

BIG J

    Right in the middle of downtown Gulfport.

GODMOTHER

    Gulfport where?

BIG J

    Gulfport, *Florida*.

GODMOTHER

    Uh-huh. Big J, tell me, how's the weather down there?

BIG J

        (*sing-song*)

    Oh, the weather's terrific, Godmother, with highs in the eighties, lows at night in the seventies, partly cloudy, and a mild breeze out of the west.

GODMOTHER

    That's nice, Big J: if you ever get tired of workin' for me, maybe you can get a job forecasting the weather. It ain't rainin', huh?

BIG J

    No, ma'am, clear & dry.

GODMOTHER

    Funny, 'cause you know where it is rainin', Big J? It's rainin' in Gulfport, Mississippi.

BIG J

>   Gulfport, Mississippi, huh. Isn't that funny: there are two Gulfports. Who'd'a thought?

GODMOTHER

>   Yeah, funny, huh? You know how I know what the weather is in Gulfport, Mississippi, Big J? 'Cause that's what Tony Mittens told me when I called him on the phone ten minutes ago.

BIG J

>   Tony Mittens is in Gulfport, Mississippi?

GODMOTHER

>   Yeah, Big J. that's where I sent him, to keep an eye on you and that genius Rocko.

BIG J

>   Well, boss, if Tony Mittens was s'posed to keep an eye on us, maybe you shoulda sent him to Gulfport, Florida.

GODMOTHER

>   You know, Big J, I woulda done that, if I had sent you and your partner to Florida. Imagine my

(MORE)

GODMOTHER (cont'd)

> surprise when Tony Mittens told me he couldn't find yous in Mississippi, WHERE I SENT YOUS!
>
> *BIG J cups his hand over the phone and glances around in a panic.*

BIG J

> Rocko, you idiot! You drove us to the wrong city!

ROCKO

> Well, that explains why we keep whackin' the wrong guy, boss, don't it?
>
> *BIG J places the phone by his ear again.*

BIG J

> Boss, we are so sorry. It's that idiot Rocko: he ain't too good with the details. But don't worry: we're gonna hustle on up to the other Gulfport and take care of the job. We got you covered.

GODMOTHER

> You got me covered, huh? How soon you gonna get there?

BIG J

    Well, it can't be too far away, right...

GODMOTHER

    It's 615 miles, Big J, and the way yous guys drive, that's a whole day. My mother drives faster than yous guys, and she's blind in one eye and can't see out of the other.

BIG J

    BIG J fusses with his bubble wrap.

    I'm sorry, boss: it's the piles. I gotta stop every hour or so and walk around, or I start to look like I got three gluteus maximuseses... maximuses...

ROCKO

    Glutei maximi, boss. It's the nominative plural in the second declension.

BIG J

        (*to ROCKO*)

    Shut up!

GODMOTHER

    You tellin' me to shut up, Big J?

BIG J

    Oh, no, ma'am. That Rocko was goin' on about somethin' from the Jeopardy. Look, we can be there in about 18 hours.

GODMOTHER

    I'll tell Tony Mittens to expect you tomorrow morning then.

BIG J

        (*equivocating*)

    Well, probably more like late Tuesday, early Wednesday. The street market here is Tuesday morning, and I'd really like to get another jar of raw honey and some fresh strawberries before we leave.

    There's a long pause.

    Hello? Godmother?

GODMOTHER

    BIG J, put Rocko on the phone.

BIG J

    Yes, ma'am.

    BIG J hands the phone to ROCKO.

        (MORE)

BIG J (cont'd)

>She wants to talk to you. Don't screw it up!
>
>>*ROCKO speaks into the phone tentatively.*

ROCKO

>Hello? Godmother?

GODMOTHER

>Rocko, you'd better get your idiot boss to Mississippi by tomorrow morning, or I'm gonna have you clip him, then I'm gonna have Tony Mittens clip you, *capisce*?

ROCKO

>Yes, ma'am, but I don't really wanna clip Big J. I like Big J, & I ain't never clipped nobody I know.

GODMOTHER

>Then won't it be a terrific idea if you get to Mississippi on time.

ROCKO

>Yes ma'am. How about Charlie Shoes? I don't really wanna clip him, neither.

GODMOTHER

    Who said anything about Charlie Shoes?

ROCKO

    It's just, with this whole cruise thing, and Mrs. Charlie...

GODMOTHER

    Rocko, you let me worry about Charlie Shoes. Now put the car in drive and point it at Mississippi. And dump them bodies before the car starts to smell.

ROCKO

    Yes, ma'am.

    The lights go down of the GODMOTHER. ROCKO hands the phone to BIG J.

BIG J

    Hello? Hello? Godmother?

    ROCKO picks the steering wheel up off the floor and starts driving.

ROCKO

    Man, for somebody who looks like a cute little old granny, the Godmother's just plain mean.

Lights down.

BIG J

    Oh, man, this is gonna make my piles flare up...

ROCKO

    Oh, that's a tricky one, boss: how many letters?

BIG J

    Just drive, Rocko. Just drive.

10. Last Rights

Synopsis: Mort & the Grim Reaper have arrived at Mort's funeral to see what people have to say about him. His adult children, Stan & Sylvie, visit with their elderly Aunt Mabel, & Mort's mistress, Consuela, all agreeing Mort wasn't much. A late arrival, a florist named Sidney, appears in drag to tell them all things about Mort they never knew.

The Cast:

MORT: the pale white ghost of a dead man (age, indeterminate) in a hospital gown, pushing an I.V. rack.

REAPER: Death, in a sharp, black suit, hat, & cane.

STAN: 40+/- years, Mort's adult son, a disappointed, middle-aged man.

SYLVIE: 40+/- years, Mort's cynical, middle-aged daughter.

AUNT MABEL: 70+/- years, Mort's elderly sister, who often seems a little confused.

CONSUELA: 55+/- years, Mort's middle-aged, Latin mistress, in a shockingly loud dress, with a clutch & a box of Kleenex.

SYDNEY: 55+/- years, a giant, cross-dressing, gay florist who seems to know Mort better than everyone else.

The Stage: Upstage center is an easel with a huge photo of Mort. Down stage left & right are several chairs. Stan & Sylvie stand behind Aunt Mabel, chatting quietly; Mort's mistress, Consuela, sits alone across from them, beside a growing pile of crumpled tissues.

ACT I

Scene 1

STAN & SYLVIE, in semi-formal attire, stand downstage left behind a row of chairs chatting (without sound); elderly AUNT MABEL sits in front of them, minding her own business. Downstage left, an over-dressed CONSUELA sits silently on a chair opposite AUNT MABEL, with a box of Kleenex & a pile of used tissue growing beside her. Enter a pallid MORT, in a hospital gown, pushing an I.V. rack, & REAPER, in a smart, black suit, hat, & cane, stage right, lingering behind the chairs stage right.

REAPER

Are you sure you want to hear this?

MORT

> (*shrugging*)
>
> It's not like I ain't heard it all before.

REAPER

> Things are different, now. You have no way of knowing what people will say.

MORT

> It's alright. This is the last time I get to see everyone, right?

REAPER

> It is.

MORT

> Well, let's go, then. I don't wanna be late for my own funeral.

REAPER

> Oh, I'm afraid *that* ship has sailed, Mort.

MORT

> Nuts! Y'know, punctuality is not an Arthur trait.

REAPER

> You're dead, Mort. Punctuality has nothing to do with it.

MORT

    Well, let's go hear my epitaph.

        MORT & the REAPER raise their arms and float past the chairs to center stage.

MORT & STAN

        (*glancing around*)

    Sheesh, not much of a crowd.

REAPER & SYLVIE

    What did you expect?

        CONSUELA starts weeping, dabbing her eyes & nose with a Kleenex. Crumpled tissues are already accumulating in the chair beside her.

MORT

    Those are my kids! And my girlfriend. Aw, poor Consuela…

STAN

    C'mon, Syl— it's not like he was a serial killer.

SYLVIE & REAPER

    There's a low bar!

SYLVIE

> I don't know why you make excuses for him. How many of *your* birthdays was he ever at? How many ball games?

STAN

> You just get used to it after a while.

SYLVIE

> Not me. I won awards— *at science fairs*! That was a big deal. My Teachers thought mom was a single mother.

STAN

> She was. She just happened to be married at the time.

SYLVIE

> He was a bad dad, Stanley, and you're like, *well, he didn't eat any livers & fava beans…*

STAN

> I'm not makin' excuses. I'm just sayin', he's dead, who cares.

REAPER

> (*wincing, to MORT*)
>
> Ow. That had to hurt.

STAN

> Where *is* Mom?

SYLVIE

> She's not comin' She says he made her miserable for the past forty-five years, & she's takin' a cruise with Aunt Maude & Uncle Harold.

STAN

> Jeez, she didn't even tell me.

SYLVIE

> She's still mad at you.

STAN

> For what?

SYLVIE

> For being a man— for being Dad's son.

STAN

> How's that my fault? *She's* the one who married him. You should tell 'er that.

SYLVIE

> I did.

STAN

> And?

SYLVIE

    She threw a Hummel at me.

STAN

    Who'd of thought she had any left?

        CONSUELA resumes weeping.

SYLVIE

    I can't believe she came here. After what she did…

STAN

    She didn't kill the marriage.

SYLVIE

    She didn't have to. Pop did that all by himself.

STAN

    At least she loved him.

SYLVIE

    For his money…

STAN

    Be nice…

        AUNT MABEL stands & hobbles up to the poster. CONSUELA resumes weeping; the Kleenex are piling up in the chair beside her.

STAN & SYLVIE

    Aw...

SYLVIE

    She's gonna say somethin'.

MORT

        (*to* REAPER)

    Aw, that's my little sister. Oy, she got *old*.

REAPER

    So, did you.

MORT

    Oh, right... duh...

        (*to* AUNT MABEL)

    Hey, kiddo...

REAPER

    She can't hear you.

MORT

    Yeah, I just get excited. I ain't seen 'er since she gone to the nursing home.

REAPER

    Shhhh... Listen.

AUNT MABEL

>Dearly beloved, we are gathered here today in the sight of god...

REAPER, MORT, STAN, & SYLVIE

>Uh oh...

AUNT MABEL

>... to witness the marriage of these two...

>>*REAPER smiles. MORT & SYLVIE covers their eyes. STAN jumps up & hurries to join AUNT MABEL. CONSUELA resumes weeping; more used Kleenex.*

MORT

>Right off the rails...

STAN

>No- no- no, Auntie Em. Here, why don't you let me help you.

>>*STAN escorts her back to her chair.*

AUNT MABEL

>>(*confused*)

>Is that you, Morty? Oh, hi— Morty, you look just like dad!

STAN

> (*loudly*)

It's me, Auntie Em: Stan. Remember me? I'm your nephew!

AUNT MABEL

Well, you don't have to shout.

SYLVIE

Here, Aunt Mabel: sit with me.

AUNT MABEL

> (*eyeing SYLVIE suspiciously*)

Who are you supposed to be?

SYLVIE

It's me, Aunt Mabel: your niece, Sylvie.

AUNT MABEL

> (*suddenly genial, taking SYLVIE's hands in her own*)

Oh, hello, dearie. Will you sit with me? We can watch the wedding together. But... but, who's going to officiate? I was going to officiate... you know, I'm a minister...

AUNT MABEL & SYLVIE

>...with the universal life church...

SYLVIE

>I know, Aunt Mabel. You presided at my marriages— both of them.

AUNT MABEL

>Well, let's hope number three is the charm. Where's that lovely fiancée of yours?
>
>>*AUNT MABEL swivels her head sharply until she espies STAN behind her.*
>
>*There* you are.

STAN

>No, we're not getting married, Auntie.

AUNT MABEL

>No?

SYLVIE

>Stan's my brother, Aunt Mabel.

AUNT MABEL

>Oh, heavens. Well, that's not right. *I'm* certainly not going to

(MORE)

AUNT MABEL (cont'd)

> marry you. You'll have to find someone else, if you're going to go in for that sort of thing.

STAN

> (*loudly*)
>
> It's dad's funeral, Auntie Em.

AUNT MABEL

> Really? Who died?

SYLVIE

> Dad died, Aunt Mabel.

AUNT MABEL

> Oh, honey: my father's passed on a long time ago.

SYLVIE

> No, *my* dad...

STAN

> (*loudly*)
>
> Your brother.

AUNT MABEL

> Oh, dear. Should I do something?

STAN

> It's okay, Aunt Mabel. We'll just sit here until the wake is over.

MORT

        (*to REAPER*)

That's my boy— he's a man now, quite a man.

REAPER

Yes, he is. I wonder where he got *that?*

MORT

I've had my moments.

    CONSUELA stops sniffling, neatens herself, and stands. Leaving her Kleenex box, she holds her clutch in front of her and approaches STAN, SYLVIE, & AUNT MABEL hesitantly.

SYLVIE

Oh, my god: she's coming over here! I can't believe she's coming over here!

STAN

Aw, c'mon...

SYLVIE

She's got *a lot* of nerve.

STAN

> C'mon, Syl. Be nice. She's obviously upset.

SYLVIE

> Ya think? We're gonna need a wheel barrow for all those soggy Kleenex.

CONSUELA

>> (*with a thick Latin accent*)
>
> Hello, excuse me. I'm your papa's special friend, Consuela.
>
>> (*glancing around*)
>
> There is not much of a crowd, huh?
>
>> (*to STAN & SYLVIE*)
>
> I just wanna say, thank you for letting me to come here. I know I'm not your mama, but Mort— he was the love of my life.

STAN

>> (*standing, extending his hand to her*)
>
> I'm Stan.

CONSUELA

> (*taking STAN's hand*)

Oh, *si*— I know you. In a way, I feel like you are my own son. You know, I never have any babies of my own.

> (*to SYLVIE*)

I'm so sorry I didn't get to know you better. I always want to, but your papa— he says no.

SYLVIE

> (*forcing a smile*)

Pleased to meet you.

> *CONSUELA plops into the chair beside SYLVIE.*

CONSUELA

You're such a pretty girl— you're both such beautiful babies. I have many fantasies about have my own, but no, Morty won't give me no babies, so all those years I park outside your school & pretend you were mine.

SYLVIE

Well, *that's* not creepy at all.

STAN

> I'm sure you would have been a wonderful mother.

CONSUELA

> I gave your papa the best years of my life. Now he is dead, and what I have? Nothing. No babies, no social security, nothing.

>> *CONSUELA bursts into tears again; STAN tries to comfort her with an awkward embrace.*

STAN

> It's okay, Miss... Consuela.

CONSUELA

> All those years he tell me, soon, Connie, I will divorce & we will marry & we will have a big family. I think sometimes he lie to me...

SYLVIE

> Yeah, welcome to the club.

>> *CONSUELA starts sobbing and lays her head on SYLVIE's shoulder. SYLVIE gives her a perfunctory pat on the shoulder.*

> There, there...

MORT

>   (*to REAPER*)

I didn't do right by her.

REAPER

It's a little late, now.

STAN

You know what, Consuela: you can be like my mom, if you like.

CONSUELA

>   (*wiping her nose on her sleeve*)

But you already have a mama.

STAN

Oh, you can't have too many mamas...

>   (*to SYLVIE*)

Can ya, Syl?

>   (*he nudges SYLVIE*)

SYLVIE

>   (*awkwardly*)

Oh, no: yeah, sure you can be like our mama.

CONSUELA

You mean it? I would *love* that.

MORT

    That's my boy. What a mensch.

STAN

    Dad didn't take care of any of us, so we'd better take care of each other.

REAPER

        (*smiling*)

    What a mensch.

    Suddenly, SYDNEY comes bustling in breathlessly from stage left, dressed in a wig, heels, & a polyester dress, with a bouquet of roses clutched in his arms. His voice is deep & masculine.

SYDNEY

    Oh, thank god you're still here. I thought I'd missed it.

STAN

    Oh, I'm sorry: this is the...

SYDNEY

    ... Mort D. Arthur funeral. I know. I'm so sorry I'm late.

AUNT MABEL

>(to STAN)

Is this the bride?

SYLVIE

And you are?

SYDNEY

Oh, sorry. I'm Sydney... the florist... friend of your dad's...

STAN

I'm Stan...

SYDNEY

I know you... and you're Sylvie, Consuela, and you must be Mort's kid sister, Mabel.

>(glancing around)

Wow! Not much of a crowd, huh.

SYLVIE

Nope, we're it.

SYDNEY

I'm sorry we haven't met until now, but I've been hearing about you all for years.

STAN

> I'm sorry... were you... were you and my dad...?

SYDNEY

> What? An item? No. No, we were just friends... *just* friends— that doesn't really say it, either. No, your dad was a pretty amazing guy, and I just wanted to share that with you.

STAN & SYLVIE

> *Our* dad? Mort Arthur?

SYDNEY

> I met your dad back in 1987—the bad old days. My friends were dying like flies. My lover was in the hospital... that's where I met Mort: he was volunteering on the AIDS ward.

STAN & SYLVIE

> *Our* dad?

SYDNEY

> We didn't have too many friends back then— I'm sure you can imagine. Your dad... he would sit with my friends for hours and tell them about your baseball games,

(MORE)

SYDNEY (cont'd)

and your science fair experiments & music recitals— I have boxes of pictures back at the shop... he was so proud of you— I don't think he ever missed a thing you did.

STAN

How come we never saw him?

SYDNEY

(*equivocating*)

Ahhh... well... uhhh... he didn't wanna make a scene with your ma. I guess they weren't getting on so well. Oh...

(*handing the roses to CONSUELA*)

These are for you. Mort helped me start my flower shop back when I was still pretty. One of the last things he did was order these.

CONSUELA

(*taking the bouquet, sniffling*)

For me?

SYDNEY

You get a bouquet once a week for,
(MORE)

SYDNEY (cont'd)

    like, forever. I got an envelope for ya, too: I think he left you his life insurance policy... it's a *lot* of money.

CONSUELA

    For me?

> *CONSUELA crushes the roses to her and resumes weeping.*

SYDNEY

    (*wrapping his arm around her shoulder*)

Honey, after these kids, you were the great love of his life. He always felt bad he didn't do better by you.

    (*to STAN & SYLVIE*)

Some of my friends have put together a little potluck for you back at my house. We were hoping you'd come join us... I mean, after the funeral— no hurry. Everyone's dying to meet you.

SYLVIE

    Meet *us*?

SYDNEY

> Honey, we may not be much, but you got a whole adopted family you've never met. I know we took your dad away from you from time to time, but Mort was there for us when no one else was. We kinda feel like we owe ya for everything he did.

STAN

> You have to forgive me: I'm a little...
>
>> (trails off, speechless)

SYLVIE

> ... Shocked. We never heard any of this.

SYDNEY

> Oh, you're gonna *love* hearin' some of our stories, then. Your dad was quite a guy.
>
>> (handing SYLVIE a card)
>
> Here's the address. When you're done here, C'mon over.

STAN & SYLVIE

>> (*standing, helping AUNT MABEL to her feet*)
>
> Oh, I think we're done here.

SYDNEY

> Great! I can show you around the flower shop. Wait 'til you see what Mort helped me build...
>
> *(he takes CONSUELA's arm & walks with her stage left)*
>
> You never saw his rainbow 'fro wig, did ya, or his giant diva sunglasses? OMG! That man knew how to make you laugh on the cloudiest day...

STAN

> *(loudly)*
>
> Auntie Em, do you wanna see some flowers?

AUNT MABEL

> *(patting STAN's hand)*
>
> You go on ahead, sweetie. I'll be along in just a second.
>
> *STAN, SYLVIE, SYDNEY, & CONSUELA exit stage left. AUNT MABEL totters over to the easel and takes down the poster of Mort, then walks directly to him.*

MORT

> She still can't see me, right?

AUNT MABEL

> (*patting MORT on the cheek*)

Ya see, Morty: you wasn't such a bad guy, after all. I'll see ya soon.

> *AUNT MABEL gives him a little kiss on the cheek, then totters stage left, carrying the poster.*

> (*to the others, off stage*)

Wait for me. Has the bride thrown the bouquet yet? Did I miss it?

> *Lights down.*

www.ingramcontent.com/pod-product-compliance
Lightning Source LLC
Chambersburg PA
CBHW061636040426
42446CB00010B/1439